MAD LIBS
WORKBOOK
GRADE 2 READING

written by Wiley Blevins

MAD LIBS
An Imprint of Penguin Random House LLC, New York

Mad Libs format and text copyright © 2020 by Penguin Random House LLC. All rights reserved.

Mad Libs concept created by Roger Price & Leonard Stern

Cover illustration by Scott Brooks
Interior illustrations by Scott Brooks, Tim Haggerty, and Jim Paillot

Designed by Dinardo Design

Published by Mad Libs,
an imprint of Penguin Random House LLC, New York.
Printed in the USA.

Visit us online at www.penguinrandomhouse.com.

ISBN 9780593096161
1 3 5 7 9 10 8 6 4 2

INSTRUCTIONS

MAD LIBS WORKBOOK is a game for kids who don't like games! It is also a review of the key reading skills for Grade 2. It has both skill practice pages and fun story pages.

RIDICULOUSLY SIMPLE DIRECTIONS:

At the top of each story page, you will find up to four columns of words, each headed by a symbol. Each symbol represents a type of word, such as a noun (naming word) or a verb (action word). The categories and symbols change from story to story. Here's an example:

MAD LIBS WORKBOOK is fun to play by yourself, but you can also play it with friends! To begin, look at the story on the page below. When you come to a blank space in the story, look at the symbol that appears underneath. Then find the same symbol on this page and pick a word that appears below the symbol. Put that word in the blank space, and cross out the word, so you don't use it again. Continue doing this throughout the story until you've filled in all the spaces. Finally, read your story aloud and laugh!

EXAMPLE:

I see a bird. It is _____ and _____ .

The bird lives in a _____ . It is shaped like a _____ .

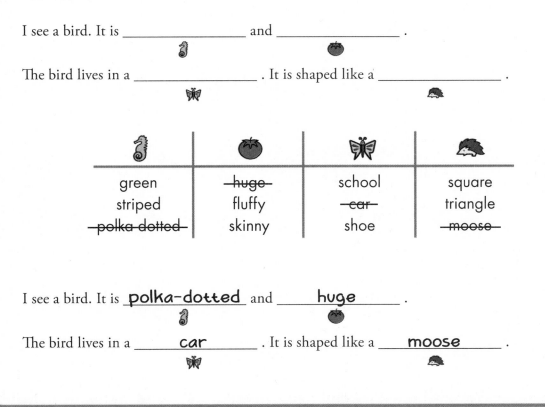

I see a bird. It is **polka-dotted** and _____**huge**_____ .

The bird lives in a _____**car**_____ . It is shaped like a _____**moose**_____ .

QUICK REVIEW

In case you haven't learned about phonics yet, here is a quick review:

There are five **VOWELS**: *a, e, i, o,* and *u.* Each vowel has a short sound and a long sound. The long sound of a vowel says its name. Sometimes the consonants *w* and *y* act as vowels when they are in vowel teams, such as *ow* (snow) and *ay* (play).

All the other letters are called **CONSONANTS**.

A **DIGRAPH** is two or more letters that together make a new sound, such as *sh* (shop) and *ch* (chin).

A **PREFIX** is a word part added to the beginning of a word, such as *un* in *unhappy.* It changes the word's meaning.

A **SUFFIX** is a word part added to the end of a word, such as *s* (bugs), *ing* (jumping), *ed* (stomped), and *ful* (playful).

In case you haven't learned about parts of speech yet, here is a quick review:

NOUNS
A **NOUN** is the name of a person, place, or thing. *Flower, kite,* and *train* are nouns.

flower

kite

train

VERBS
A **VERB** is an action word. *Draw, spin,* and *share* are verbs.

draw

spin

share

ADJECTIVES
An **ADJECTIVE** describes a person, place, or thing. *Green, happy,* and *muddy* are adjectives.

green

happy

muddy

PHONICS

Short Vowels

Short vowels can be spelled many ways.

bl**a**ck

sh**i**p

fr**o**g

dr**u**m

sl**e**d

h**ea**d

Add a short vowel spelling to finish each picture name.

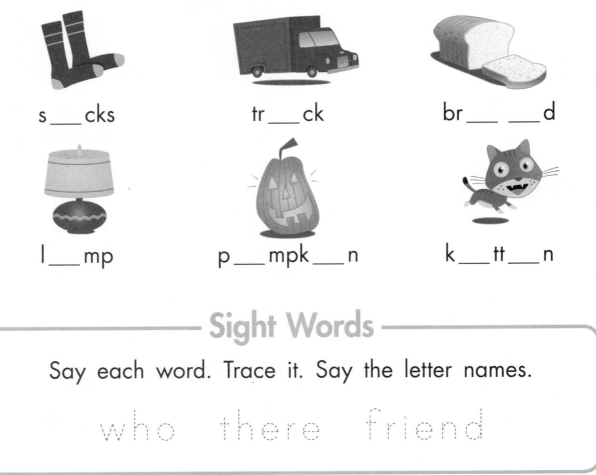

s ___ cks

tr ___ ck

br ___ ___ d

l ___ mp

p ___ mpk ___ n

k ___ tt ___ n

Sight Words

Say each word. Trace it. Say the letter names.

who   there   friend

🍕	🌱	🦴	🍌
flat	stomped	mud	van
grumpy	wiggled	frogs	slug
Swiss	jumped	socks	nut
smelly	clucked	pencils	bobsled
well-fed	burped	chicken pox	grasshopper

Little Red Hen

There once lived a little red and _____ hen. She had
(🍕)

to bake some _____ . "Who will help me?" she asked.
(🦴)

The hen _____ to her friend the _____ .
(🌱)   (🍌)

"Will you help me?" she asked. "No way!" said her friend. The hen

then _____ to her friend the _____ . "Will
(🌱)   (🍌)

you help me?" she asked. "Not me!" said her friend. Next, the hen

_____ to her friend the _____ . "Will
(🌱)   (🍌)

you help me?" she asked. "Never!" said her friend. "That's

it!" the hen _____ . "I will bake the bread
(🌱)

and get new friends." And that is exactly what she did.

PHONICS

Blends

When two consonants are together in a word, we often hear the sound of both letters.

__fl__ower   __st__op   __pr__incess

Add two letters to finish each picture name.

___ ___een

___ ___ane

___ ___unk

___ ___in

___ ___agon

___ ___elling

Sight Words

Say each word. Trace it. Say the letter names.

over   lived   already

🦋	🥕	🦆	👕
stinky	pretzel	squeaked	trick
sweaty	crayon	blasted	flip
hunky	clown	fainted	flush
tiny	flea	slimed	freeze

The Troll Under the Bridge

One day, a _____ wanted to cross a bridge over a pond.
🥕

Under that bridge lived a _____ and _____
🦋   🦋

troll. Stamp, stomp, stamp. He _____ over the bridge.
🦆

"Who tramps over my bridge?" yelled the troll. "Stop or I will

_____ you!" But he had already crossed the bridge.
👕

On the next day, a sleepy _____ wanted to cross the
🥕

bridge. Stamp, stomp, stamp. He _____ over the bridge.
🦆

"Who tramps over my bridge?" yelled the troll. "Stop or

I will _____ you! Oh, never mind.
👕

Nobody listens to me anyway!" And with that,

the troll _____ away.
🦆

Digraphs

When two or more consonants are together in a word, they sometimes make a new sound.

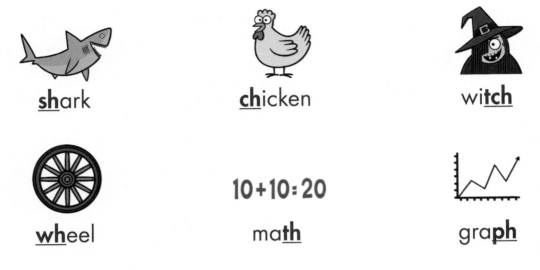

shark

chicken

wi**tch**

wheel

10+10=20

ma**th**

gra**ph**

Add two or more letters to finish each picture name.

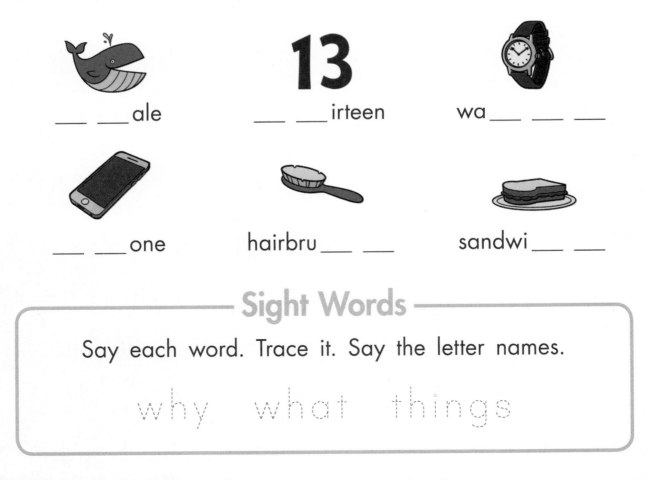

___ ___ale

___ ___irteen

wa ___ ___ ___

___ ___one

hairbru ___ ___

sandwi ___ ___

Sight Words

Say each word. Trace it. Say the letter names.

why   what   things

🍅	🐟	🌴	🐋
chips	moth	cheeseburger	bathe
ships	peach	chicken	fish
benches	chair	big ship	paint
children	Whiskers	dish	shave
bathtubs	Thunderbolt	watch	stretch

A Day at the Beach

My family went on a day trip. **Where?** To the beach. **When?** Last spring!

Why? Dad likes to throw things in the sand, such as _____
🍅

and _____ so our pet _____ can fetch
🍅   🐟

them. And Mom? Splash! Mom likes to jump into the water with

her _____ and _____ . **What** did I do at
🌴   🐋

the beach? I spotted a whale with a _____ in its
🌴

mouth. The whale crashed against the beach. Its thick tail

swished back and forth. Dad said it looked hungry and

thirsty, so he threw some _____ at it.
🍅

What a fun day!

 **PHONICS**

Final e

When a word ends in **e**, the vowel before it and the **e** work together to say the vowel's name.

k<u>i</u>t

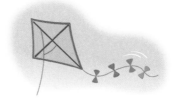

k<u>ite</u>

Add a **vowel** (a, e, i, o, u) and **e** (at the end) to finish each picture name.

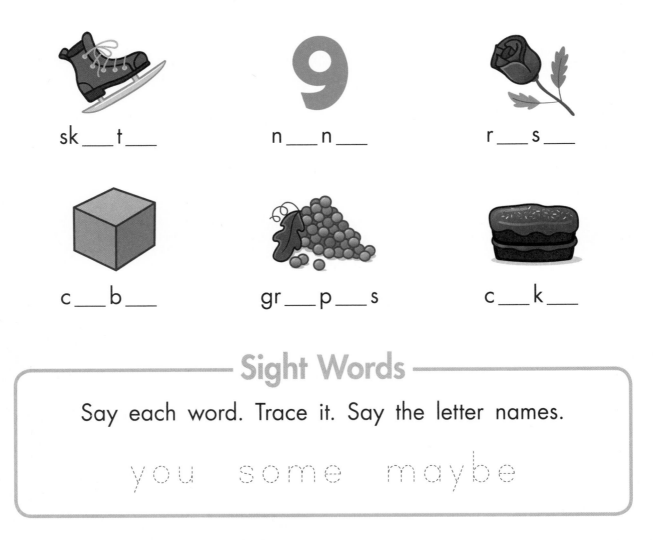

sk___t___   n___n___   r___s___

c___b___   gr___p___s   c___k___

Sight Words

Say each word. Trace it. Say the letter names.

you   some   maybe

🍍	🍡	❄️	🐶
muddy	lice	kite	wave at
gooey	paste	bike	shake
stale	noses	smile	play with
shapeless	grapes	grave	chase
full of mice	sunshine	porcupine	explode

Let's Bake a Cake

It's time to bake a cake for your best friend. Yay! First, you must

get the yummy ingredients. You will need to use _____
                                                            🍡

and _____ and maybe some _____ . Next,
        🍡   🍡

you will need to decide on the shape of the cake. It can be shaped

like a _____ or a _____ . Make it fun.
            ❄️   ❄️

After that, you will _____ all the ingredients.
                            🐶

Finally, it's time to place the cake in the oven. Let it

bake nine or ten minutes, but don't serve it until it's

_____ and _____ .
        🍍   🍍

Long a

The **long a** sound can be spelled many ways.

tr**ai**n

gr**ay**

sl**eigh**

t**a**ble

f**a**c**e**

Add **ai**, **ay**, **eigh**, **a**, or **a_e** to finish each picture name.

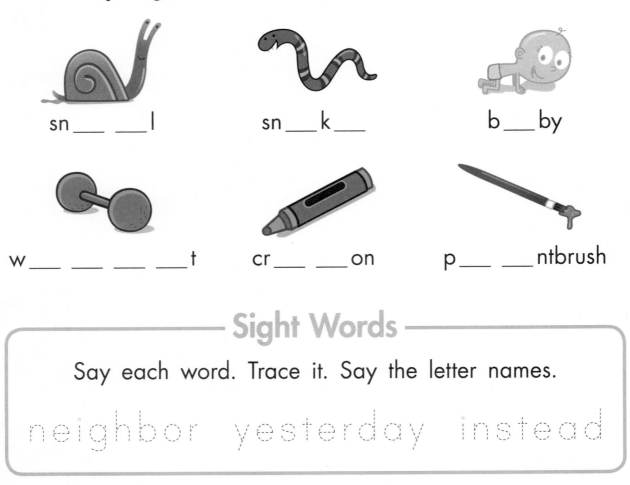

sn ___ ___ l

sn ___ k ___

b ___ by

w ___ ___ ___ ___ t

cr ___ ___ on

p ___ ___ ntbrush

Sight Words

Say each word. Trace it. Say the letter names.

neighbor   yesterday   instead

🌶	🌴	🍍	🍉
a cave	snail	pale gray	blue jay
someplace	sleigh	lacy	mermaid
Spain	whale	caged	ice tray
space	rake	runaway	skate
Ukraine	subway	tattletale	Great Dane

Breaking News!

Gail and her neighbor went on a great vacation to _____

🌶

last Sunday. It was a holiday treat! They took a _____ to get

🌴

there and paid a _____ _____ to give them

🍍 🌴

a tour of the place. "Why is this breaking news?" you ask. Yesterday,

Gail complained she had a stomachache. The doctor did an X-ray to

figure out the problem. It turns out, she ate a _____

🍍

_____ on the trip. "Hey! No way!" exclaimed

🍉

the doctor. "Burp!" said Gail. "What can I do, Doctor?"

"Stay home on your next holiday," he said. "And next time,

try eating a/an _____ instead."

🍉

PHONICS

Long e

The **long e** sound can be spelled many ways.

str**ee**t

l**ea**f

f**ie**ld

w**e**

k**ey**

happ**y**

Add **ee**, **ea**, **ie**, **e**, **ey**, or **y** to finish each picture name.

b___ ___ch

3

thr___ ___

monk___ ___

p___ ___ce

mudd___

b___tw___ ___n

Sight Words

Say each word. Trace it. Say the letter names.

people   many   with

🧁	🦆	🍌	🦔
sticky	freeze	jelly bean	leap on
sneezy	squeeze	treehouse	squeal at
squeaky	teach	tepee	feast on
dreamy	beep at	fire chief	shield
peewee	tease	parakeet	free

King or Queen for a Day

If I were king or queen for a day, I would do many _____

things. I would _____ or _____ a

_____ . It seems like an easy thing to do and in keeping

with my royal rights. If I were king or queen for a day, I might try

many _____ things, too. I might _____ a

_____ . Not many people can say they did that. Guaranteed!

If I were king or queen for a day, I would make friends with

a _____ and spend a _____

day together. Oh, you wouldn't believe the things I'd do if

I were king or queen for a day. What would you do?

PHONICS

Long o

The **long o** sound can be spelled many ways.

g**oa**t

sn**ow**man

r**o**p**e**

g**o**

t**oe**s

Add **oa**, **ow**, **o_e**, **o**, or **oe** to finish each picture name.

st___n___s

gh___st

thr___ ___t

rainb___ ___

tic-tac-t___ ___

buffal___

Sight Words

Say each word. Trace it. Say the letter names.

our   too   doesn't

🐋	🍅	🦋	🍕
so-so	mice	noses	egg roll
snowy	ice cream	toes	ghost
yellow	scarecrows	roses	radio
glowing	rainbows	phones	flagpole
soapy	bones	goats	globe

Let's Play Soccer

Is it ever too cold outside to play soccer? Our coach certainly doesn't

think so—even without a ball. One _____ day, he said,
🐋

"Let's go play, team!" We should have known it was better to stay in

our roasty-toasty _____ . The snow, shaped like little
🍕

_____ and _____ , tumbled all around us.
🍅 🍅

It also fell on our _____ and began to
🦋

grow and grow. "Go, go, goal!" yelled our coach.

"Kick the _____ ." But all we
🍕

could do was throw it. Did we score a goal?

No! But we set another goal . . . to go home.

Long i

The **long i** sound can be spelled many ways.

br**igh**t   t**ie**   cr**y**

k**i**t**e**   ch**i**ld

Add **igh**, **ie**, **y**, **i_e**, or **i** to finish each picture name.

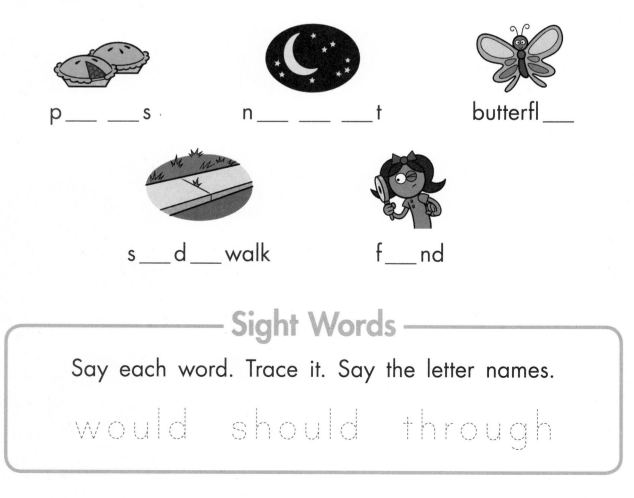

p___ ___s   n___ ___ ___t   butterfl___

s___d___walk   f___nd

Sight Words

Say each word. Trace it. Say the letter names.

would   should   through

🥕	🍦	🧁	🍍
wide	bride	fried	tie
unkind	slice of pie	childlike	beehive
wise	spy	mild	knife
mighty	french fry	dried	bike
wild	valentine	terrified	reptile

What Can Fly?

Can a/an _____ _____ fly high in the sky?
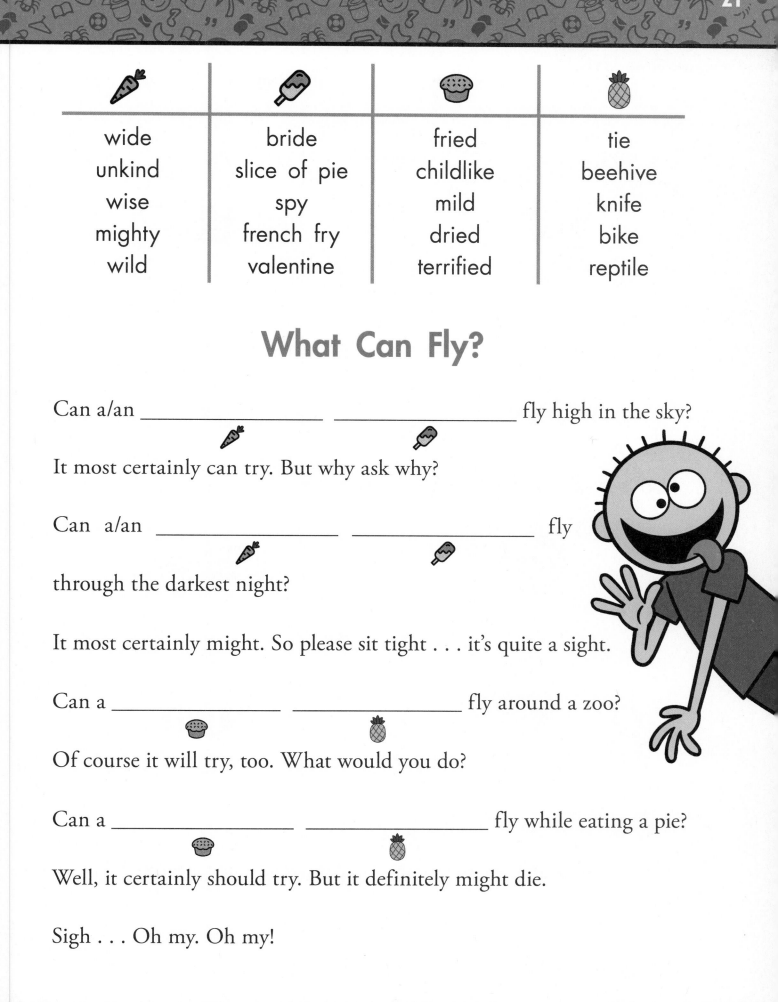

It most certainly can try. But why ask why?

Can a/an _____ _____ fly

through the darkest night?

It most certainly might. So please sit tight . . . it's quite a sight.

Can a _____ _____ fly around a zoo?

Of course it will try, too. What would you do?

Can a _____ _____ fly while eating a pie?

Well, it certainly should try. But it definitely might die.

Sigh . . . Oh my. Oh my!

Long u

The **long u** sound can be spelled many ways.

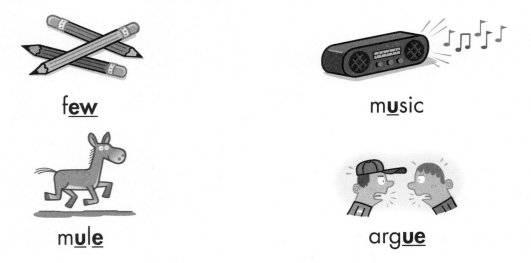

f**ew**

m**u**sic

m**u**l**e**

arg**ue**

Add **ew**, **u**, **u_e**, or **ue** to finish each picture name.

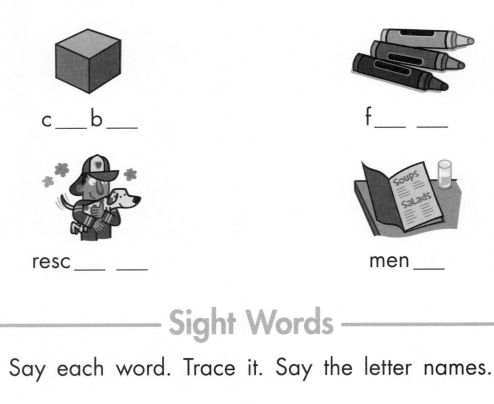

c___b___

f___ ___

resc___ ___

men ___

Sight Words

Say each word. Trace it. Say the letter names.

most   won't   another

🐶	🔵	👕	🐟
mule	uniform	hairy	For reals
cube	menu	silly	Don't argue
pickle	tail	useless	Let's continue
carrot	feather hat	delicious	Who knew

At the Museum

Dear Mr. Principal,

Our class went to the most _____ 👕 museum on Earth. We

saw a few things you won't believe! Humans are quite strange creatures!

In one room stood a _____ 🐶 wearing a _____ 🔵 .

_____ 🐟 ! In another room sat a huge _____ 🐶

with a _____ 🔵 . _____ 🐟 ! In the last room, we

heard a _____ 🐶 playing beautiful music. That's when we did

a U-turn, got lost, and our teacher had to rescue us. Our

advice is to review the website for any museum on

Earth before you visit. _____ 🐟 !

Sincerely, Your Students

PHONICS

r-Controlled Vowels
er, ir, ur

The letters **er**, **ir**, and **ur** all stand for the same sounds.

sh**ir**t

t**ur**tle

f**er**n

Add **er**, **ir**, or **ur** to finish each picture name.

sk___ ___t

f___ ___st

p___ ___ple

moth___ ___

Sight Words

Say each word. Trace it. Say the letter names.

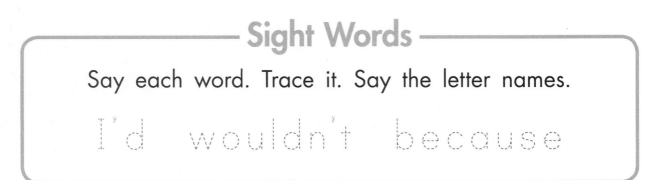

I'd   wouldn't   because

🍉	🌴	🌶️	🦋
purple	fern	curse	turtle
curious	squirrel	flirt with	sunburn
purring	turkey	circle	purse
blurry	mother	return	germ
nervous	nurse	observe	jerk

Birthday Surprise

Which do you think would be the best birthday surprise?

Option 1: I'd like to receive a _____ skirt and a
🍉

_____ shirt for my _____ . That's because
🍉   🌴

I like to play dress up. I've seen a _____ in a skirt looking
🌴

like a blur when it turns and twirls. That would be perfect!

Option 2: I'd like to _____ a _____
🌶️   🦋

so I can learn more about it. I also have the urge to purge

my old stuff. I could _____ my
🌶️

_____ in order to get a better one.
🦋

What person wouldn't?

r-Controlled Vowels
or, ore, ar

When a vowel is followed by the letter **r**, the **r** affects the vowel sound. It is neither long nor short.

c**or**n

c**ar**

The "or" sounds can also be spelled <u>ore</u> as in **more** and <u>oar</u> as in **roaring**.

Add **or** or **ar** to finish each picture name.

b___ ___n   h___ ___n   f___ ___k

st___ ___s   f___ ___mer   thunderst___ ___m

Sight Words

Say each word. Trace it. Say the letter names.

do   more   put

🐟	🧁	🌴	🍅
oar	hot dog	dancers	thunderstorm
guitar	pitchfork	lions	tractor
horn	pork chop	unicorns	cigar
shark	barn	starfish	Mozart
leotard	tart	farmers	stork

Park Carnival

There's a carnival in New York's Central Park this weekend! There

is no charge to enter. What can you see and do there? For starters,

grab a/an _____ and hop in a boat. For more fun, visit
🐟

the zoo, where you'll hear the _____ roar. Explore
🌴

the food carts. You can buy a _____ or a yummy
🧁

burger. Then head over to the outdoor shows to watch

the _____ and _____
🌴 🌴

perform. If you like sports, race to the ballpark. Put on a

uniform and play with one of the teams. But don't stay after

dark. There's a report that a large _____ is coming at nine.
🍅

PHONICS

r-Controlled Vowels
air, are, ear

The letters **air**, **are**, and **ear** all stand for the same sounds.

h**air**

silverw**are**

p**ear**

Add **air**, **are**, or **ear** to finish each picture name.

squ___ ___ ___

ch___ ___ ___

b___ ___ ___s

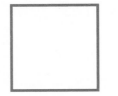

st___ ___ ___case

underw___ ___ ___

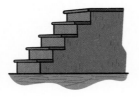

sh___ ___ ___

Sight Words

Say each word. Trace it. Say the letter names.

one   once   there

🦋	🦴	🌊	🍦
golden	bare	soup	bath
pink	fair	jam	swim
fuzzy	thorny	pickles	break
skinny	squishy	rocks	flight

The Three Bears

Once upon a time, a _____ -haired girl walked deep
🦋

into the forest. She spotted the house of three _____
🦴

bears. She knocked on the door, but no one was there. She didn't

care. She burst through the door. Three bowls of _____
🦴

_____ sat on the table. She found a comfy chair
🌊

to sit in and slurped them down. Then she ran upstairs to take a

_____ on a bed. She tried each bed to see which was just
🍦

right. One was too _____ and lumpy. Another was too
🦋

soft and _____ . The last bed was perfect.
🦴

So she fell fast asleep, and that's where the three bears

found her. What did they do? They ate her.

 **PHONICS**

Diphthongs oi, oy; ou, ow

Some vowel sounds feel like they move around in your mouth.

cowb**oy**

b**oi**l

m**ou**th

cl**ow**n

Add **oy**, **oi**, **ou**, or **ow** to finish each picture name.

s___ ___l   dogh___ ___se   t___ ___s

br___ ___n   cr___ ___n   c___ ___ns

Sight Words

Say each word. Trace it. Say the letter names.

girls   come   might

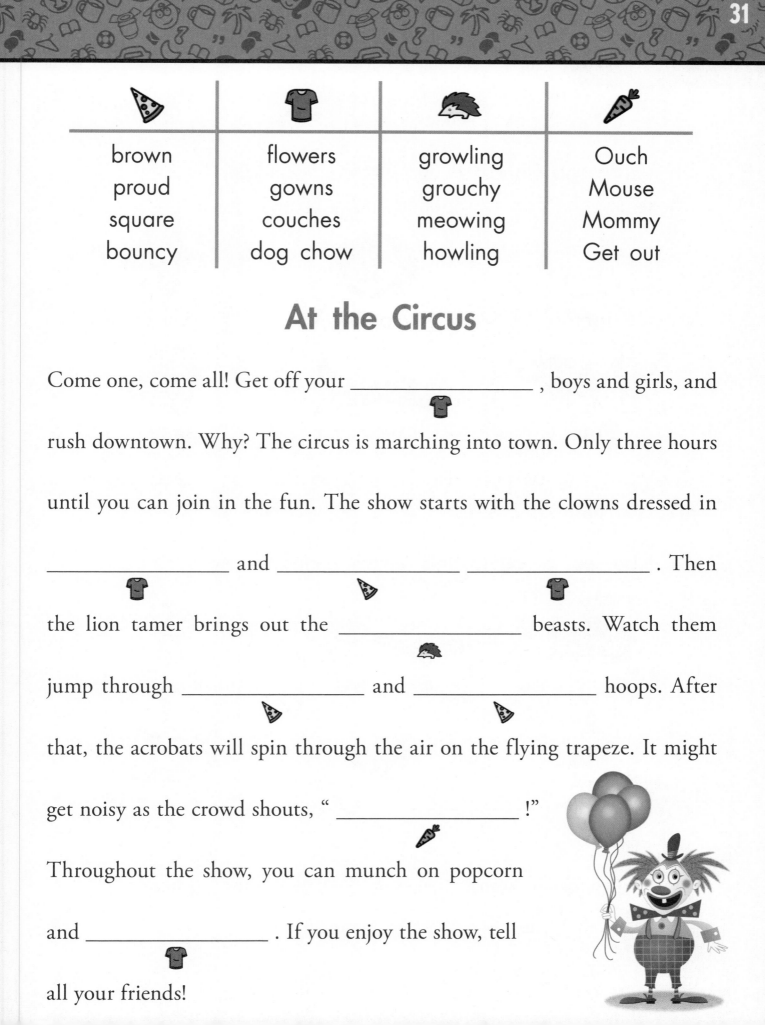			
brown	flowers	growling	Ouch
proud	gowns	grouchy	Mouse
square	couches	meowing	Mommy
bouncy	dog chow	howling	Get out

At the Circus

Come one, come all! Get off your _____ , boys and girls, and

rush downtown. Why? The circus is marching into town. Only three hours

until you can join in the fun. The show starts with the clowns dressed in

_____ and _____ _____ . Then

the lion tamer brings out the _____ beasts. Watch them

jump through _____ and _____ hoops. After

that, the acrobats will spin through the air on the flying trapeze. It might

get noisy as the crowd shouts, " _____ !"

Throughout the show, you can munch on popcorn

and _____ . If you enjoy the show, tell

all your friends!

PHONICS

Variant Vowels oo

The letters **oo** stand for two different sounds.
These sounds can be spelled many ways.

f**oo**t   m**oo**n   bl**ue**

gr**ou**p   n**ew**   J**u**n**e**

The "oo" sounds can also be spelled **ould** as in **could** and
u as in **put**.

Add **oo**, **ue**, or **ou** to finish each picture name.

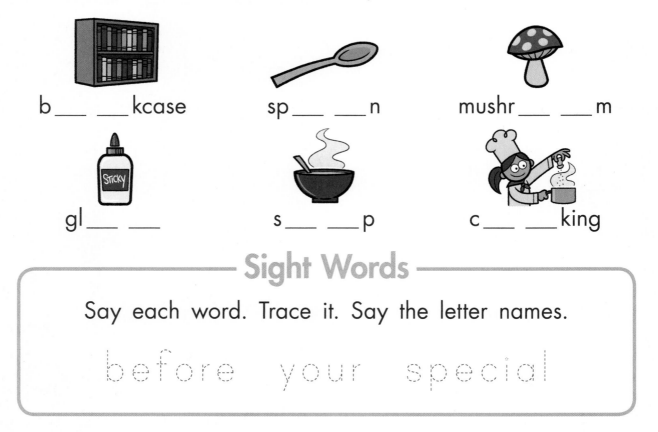

b___ ___kcase   sp___ ___n   mushr___ ___m

gl___ ___   s___ ___p   c___ ___king

Sight Words

Say each word. Trace it. Say the letter names.

before your special

❄	🌶	🐋	🏐
tooth	kangaroo	glue	zoom
balloon	shampoo	prunes	ooze
cuckoo	spoons	cocoons	chew
flute	moose	brooms	moo

The Hidden Cookbook

Ruth found a hidden cookbook under a _____ in her ❄

kitchen. When she opened the book, it was filled with recipes she'd never

seen before. One group of recipes used things like _____ 🌶

and _____ to make tasty soups. Another group used 🌶

_____ and _____ to make stew. Grab a spoon 🐋 🐋

and join her! But don't get too full. Save room for the yummy desserts.

Invite your friends to cook after school. Make toasted _____ 🐋

for your teacher or baked _____ for 🌶

your family. If you run out of the special ingredients,

_____ over to the store and get some more. 🏐

Who knew cooking could be such fun?

Variant Vowels
au, aw, augh, ough, al

The vowel sound in **all** can be spelled many ways.

dr<u>aw</u>   s<u>au</u>sage   f<u>a</u>ll

t<u>al</u>k   s<u>al</u>t

The "aw" sounds can also be spelled <u>**ough**</u> as in **bought** and <u>**augh**</u> as in **taught**.

Add **aw**, **au**, or **al** to finish each picture name.

sidew___ ___k   cr___ ___ling

baseb___ ___l   l___ ___nching

— **Sight Words** —

Say each word. Trace it. Say the letter names.

friend   everyone   probably

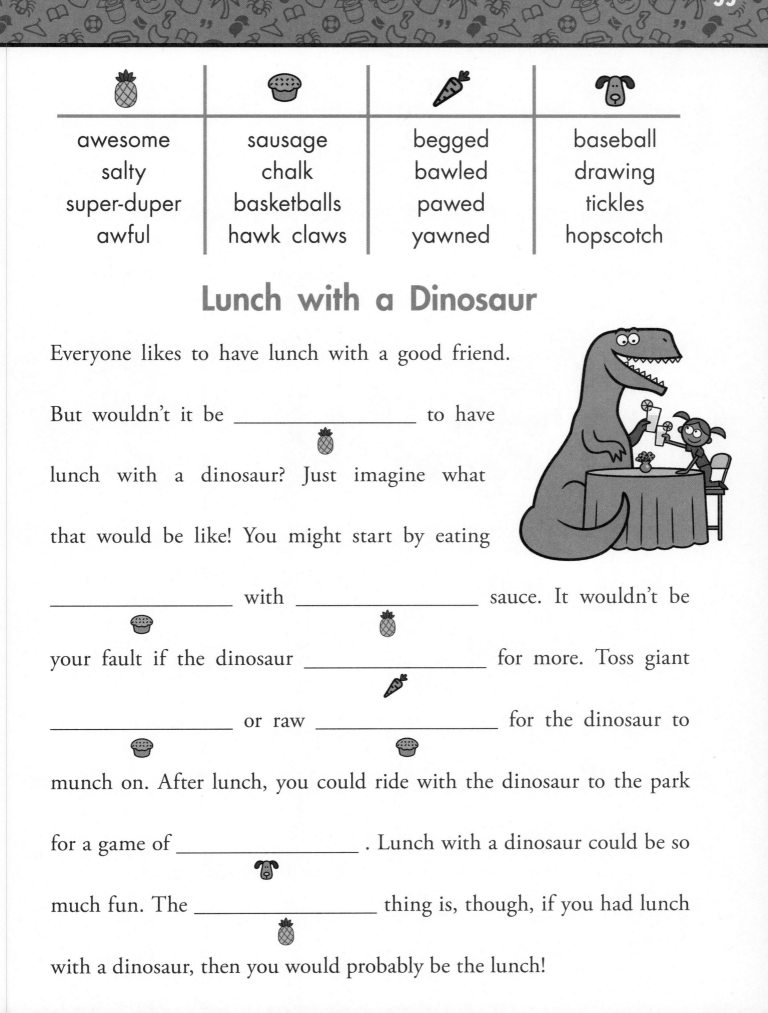 🍍	🧁	🥕	🐶
awesome	sausage	begged	baseball
salty	chalk	bawled	drawing
super-duper	basketballs	pawed	tickles
awful	hawk claws	yawned	hopscotch

Lunch with a Dinosaur

Everyone likes to have lunch with a good friend.

But wouldn't it be _____ 🍍 to have

lunch with a dinosaur? Just imagine what

that would be like! You might start by eating

_____ 🧁 with _____ 🍍 sauce. It wouldn't be

your fault if the dinosaur _____ 🥕 for more. Toss giant

_____ 🧁 or raw _____ 🧁 for the dinosaur to

munch on. After lunch, you could ride with the dinosaur to the park

for a game of _____ 🐶 . Lunch with a dinosaur could be so

much fun. The _____ 🍍 thing is, though, if you had lunch

with a dinosaur, then you would probably be the lunch!

WRITING: Spelling and Grammar

Inflectional Endings
s, ed, ing

You can add **s**, **ed**, or **ing** to a verb, or action word.

| stomp | stomp**s** | stomp**ed** | stomp**ing** |

Add **s**, **ed**, and **ing** to each word. Say a sentence for each word.

	Add **s**	Add **ed**	Add **ing**
act	_____	_____	_____
clean	_____	_____	_____
paint	_____	_____	_____

Sight Words

Say each word. Trace it. Say the letter names.

different   children   women

🍉	🦄	🍌	🐟
horses	fuzzy	poodle	eating
chickens	feathered	lizard	smelling
eggplants	monkey	yogurt	toasting
geese	flowered	dentist	licking

Now and Long Ago

Time changes many things. Long ago, people used carts with

_____ 🍉 to get around. Today, we ride in

cars. Long ago, men wore hats and _____ 🦄

suits. Women also wore _____ 🦄 hats and

long dresses with _____ 🍉 underneath. Long ago,

children played games like _____ 🍌 , hopscotch,

and marbles. Today, children can be found _____ 🐟

games on computers and cell phones. Long ago, many students

from different grades learned in the same classroom with the same

_____ 🍌 . Today, each classroom has a different teacher

with students _____ 🐟 subjects like math and science.

Inflectional Endings with Spelling Changes

When you add **s**, **es**, **ed**, or **ing** to a word, you sometimes have to change the spelling before adding the ending.

1. Double the final consonant

stop   stops   sto**pp**ed   sto**pp**ing

2. Drop e

save   saves   saved   sav**ing**

3. Change y to i

cry   cr**i**es   cr**i**ed   crying

Add **s**, **ed**, and **ing** to each word.

	Add **s** or **es**	Add **ed**	Add **ing**
tap			
bake			
try			

Sight Words

Say each word. Trace it. Say the letter names.

brother   my   something

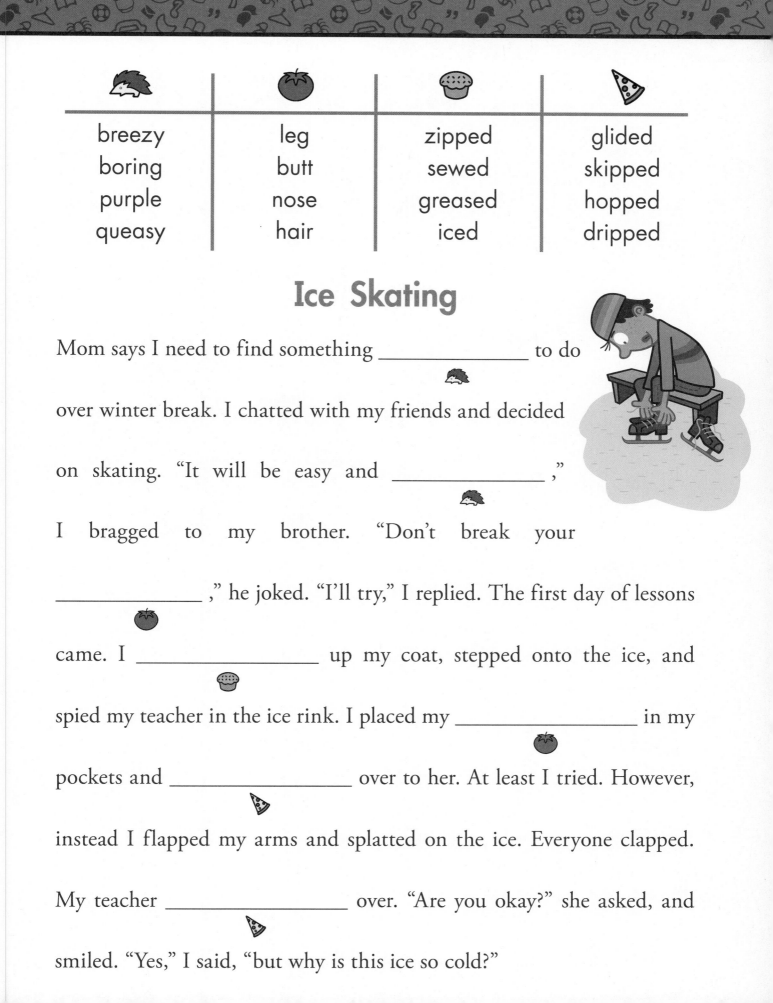			
breezy	leg	zipped	glided
boring	butt	sewed	skipped
purple	nose	greased	hopped
queasy	hair	iced	dripped

Ice Skating

Mom says I need to find something _____ to do

over winter break. I chatted with my friends and decided

on skating. "It will be easy and _____,"

I bragged to my brother. "Don't break your

_____," he joked. "I'll try," I replied. The first day of lessons

came. I _____ up my coat, stepped onto the ice, and

spied my teacher in the ice rink. I placed my _____ in my

pockets and _____ over to her. At least I tried. However,

instead I flapped my arms and splatted on the ice. Everyone clapped.

My teacher _____ over. "Are you okay?" she asked, and

smiled. "Yes," I said, "but why is this ice so cold?"

WRITING: Spelling and Grammar

Irregular Plural Nouns

A **plural** word is more than one of something.
Most naming words, or nouns, add **s** or **es** to make it plural.
However, some plural words do not. We call them irregular.

Regular

1 cat   2 cat**s**

1 box   2 box**es**

Irregular

1 man   2 men

1 mouse 2 mice

Write the plural of each word.

1 foot   2 _____   1 woman   2 _____

1 knife   2 _____   1 child   2 _____

1 tooth   2 _____   1 sheep   2 _____

Sight Words

Say each word. Trace it. Say the letter names.

been long pictures

🔵	🌴	🦴	👕
lake	cage	square	lice
noodle	balloon	pink	mice
tree	bubble	crunchy	elves
shoe	bathroom	gooey	teeth

At the Zoo

Come see my favorite zoo! It is located in the middle of a giant

_____ . When I walked in, I saw a _____
🔵

filled with _____ _____ . Beside
🌴

it was a _____ filled with _____
🦴　　　　　　　　　　　　　　　👕

_____ and sitting on a _____ . Men, women,
🌴　　　　　　　　　　　　　　🔵
👕

and children gathered around to take pictures. Snap! Snap! Selfie!

I walked around so long my feet began to hurt. So I decided to eat

some loaves of bread filled with _____ and
👕

shaped like _____ . What a great
👕

snack! I highly recommend a visit to this zoo

the next time you're in town.

WRITING: Spelling and Grammar

Collective Nouns

A **collective noun** is used to name a group of people, animals, or things.

A **crowd** of people   A **crew** of sailors

A **herd** of cows   A **flock** of geese

A **stack** of books   A **heap** of trash

Add a collective noun to finish each picture name.
Use **batch**, **herd**, **set**, or **class**.

A _____ of elephants

A _____ of bowls

A _____ of cookies

A _____ of students

Sight Words

Say each word. Trace it. Say the letter names.

beautiful   move   mountain

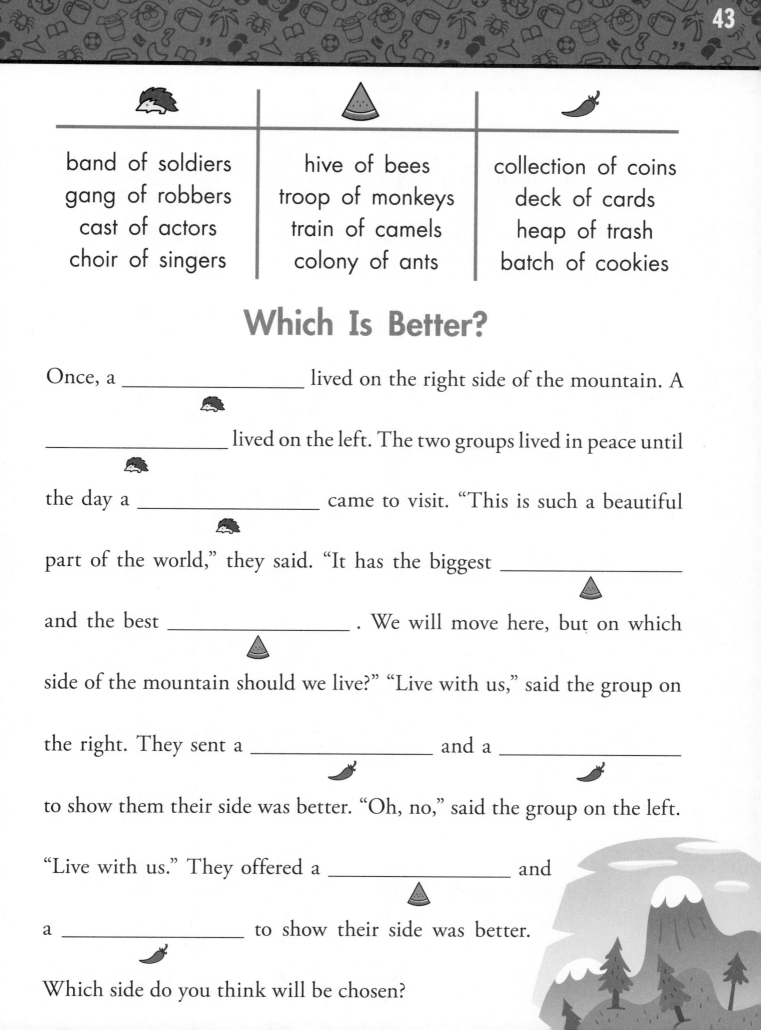		
band of soldiers	hive of bees	collection of coins
gang of robbers	troop of monkeys	deck of cards
cast of actors	train of camels	heap of trash
choir of singers	colony of ants	batch of cookies

Which Is Better?

Once, a _____ lived on the right side of the mountain. A

_____ lived on the left. The two groups lived in peace until

the day a _____ came to visit. "This is such a beautiful

part of the world," they said. "It has the biggest _____

and the best _____ . We will move here, but on which

side of the mountain should we live?" "Live with us," said the group on

the right. They sent a _____ and a _____

to show them their side was better. "Oh, no," said the group on the left.

"Live with us." They offered a _____ and

a _____ to show their side was better.

Which side do you think will be chosen?

Reflexive Pronouns

Reflexive pronouns are words ending in **self** or **selves**.

myself	yourself	himself
herself	oneself	itself
ourselves	yourselves	themselves

Use a word from above to finish each sentence.

He helped _____ to a big bowl of soup.

We saved _____ from doing all that work.

I looked at _____ in the bathroom mirror.

They bought _____ new uniforms for
the big game.

Sight Words

Say each word. Trace it. Say the letter names.

caught   sure   today

🍍	🍡	🌴	🦋
cry	snails	napping	Oh my!
sneeze	butter	dancing	Is it Friday?
pass out	pickles	baking	Turtles!
sing	thumbtacks	jumping rope	Who am I?

The Substitute

Today, my class had a substitute teacher. I told myself I wouldn't

_____ , but I did. The substitute teacher helped herself
🍍

to Mr. Robin's jar of _____ and ate while
🍡

we read our books and wrote our stories. During math,

we taught ourselves fractions. Why? Our substitute

teacher was _____ on the desk. After lunch,
🌴

we caught her _____ in the hallway. The
🌴

principal whispered to himself, "_____" Then he
🦋

gave himself a bathroom pass and slipped away. That's when everyone

began to _____ about the _____ . Having a
🍍 🍡

substitute teacher sure is fun, but I can't wait for Mr. Robin to return!

Verbs

Verbs are action words.
Present tense verbs tell about things
happening now. Past tense verbs tell
about things that already happened.

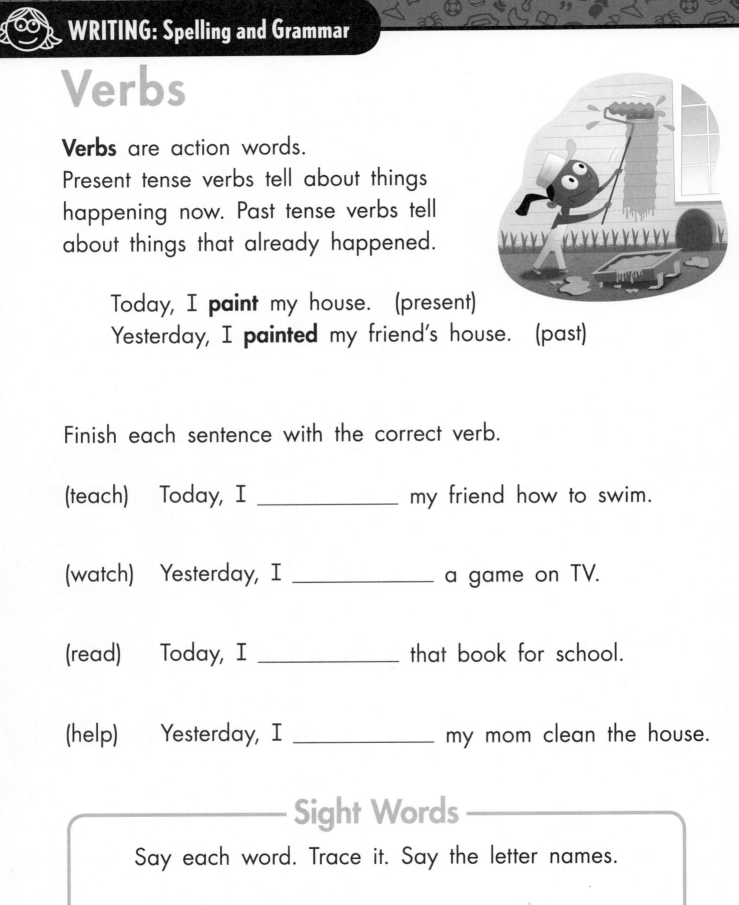

Today, I **paint** my house. (present)
Yesterday, I **painted** my friend's house. (past)

Finish each sentence with the correct verb.

(teach)   Today, I _____ my friend how to swim.

(watch)   Yesterday, I _____ a game on TV.

(read)   Today, I _____ that book for school.

(help)   Yesterday, I _____ my mom clean the house.

Sight Words

Say each word. Trace it. Say the letter names.

two   were   again

🐚	❄️	🥕	🍌
swim	dashed	turtles	witch
crawl	zoomed	ghosts	teacher
burp	giggled	beetles	senator
sing	marched	dancers	penguin

Hansel and Gretel

Hansel and Gretel were two _____ who got lost in the 🥕

forest one day. We all know why and it's too sad to repeat. "We need

to _____ to get out of here," said Hansel. "Or we 🐚

can _____," said Gretel. Just then, a cold breeze swept 🐚

through the forest. "_____!" yelled Hansel. The two 🐚

_____ deeper into the forest until they came to the home ❄️

of a _____ who had six pet _____ . "Come 🍌 🥕

in," said the homeowner. "I will feed you a tasty _____ ." 🍌

When Hansel and Gretel heard this, they slammed

the door and _____ deeper into the ❄️

forest. They were never seen or heard from again.

WRITING: Spelling and Grammar

Irregular Past-Tense Verbs

Most past tense verbs end in **ed**.

> Today, I **walk** to the store. (present)
> Yesterday, I **walked** to the store. (past)

However, some verbs do not.
We call these irregular.

> Today, I **run** in the park. (present)
> Yesterday, I **ran** in the park. (past)

Finish each sentence with the past tense form of each verb.

(bite)   Yesterday, I _____ into the apple.

(send)   Yesterday, I _____ an e-mail to my friend.

(buy)   Yesterday, I _____ a new soccer ball.

(drink)   Yesterday, I _____ a big glass of milk.

Sight Words

Say each word. Trace it. Say the letter names.

thought   taught   possible

🐋	🍉	🍕	🦆
squeaky	monster	drove	airplane
smelly	giraffe	grew	subway
burping	doctor	bit	camel
roaring	pickle	fell	crocodile

What a Day!

Yesterday was a day the Sampson twins will never forget. They

woke up when they heard a _____ noise. It was a
🐋

_____ that _____ into the house. After that,
🍉   🍕

they rode a/an _____ to the store and bought a board game
🦆

to play. Unfortunately, they lost the game on the _____ as
🦆

they went home. The twins thought their day couldn't get weirder, but

they understood anything was possible. At home, a _____
🐋

_____ _____ into their kitchen.
🍉   🍕

The twins taught their guest how to bake cookies.

Their guest sent them to bed, and that was the

end of a day they'll never forget.

WRITING: Spelling and Grammar

Adjectives

An **adjective** is a describing word.
It tells more about something.

a cat

a **little** cat

a **black** cat

Add adjectives to finish each sentence.

The _____ dog barks.

The dress is _____ .

The _____ boy has a _____ coat.

Sight Words

Say each word. Trace it. Say the letter names.

across   bought   enough

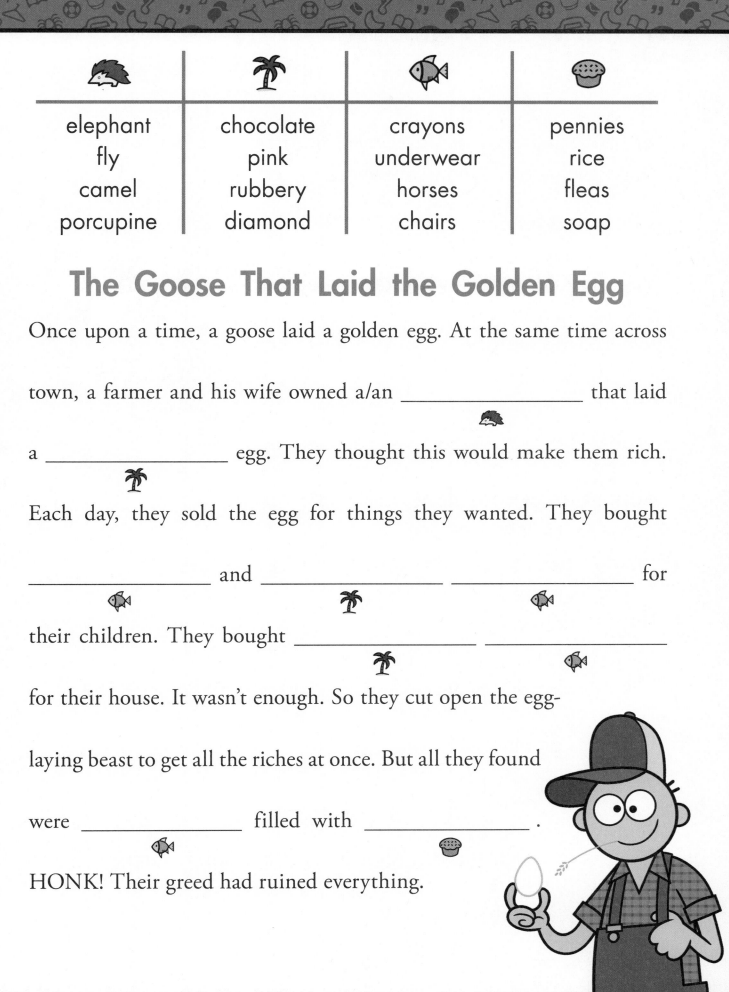			
elephant	chocolate	crayons	pennies
fly	pink	underwear	rice
camel	rubbery	horses	fleas
porcupine	diamond	chairs	soap

The Goose That Laid the Golden Egg

Once upon a time, a goose laid a golden egg. At the same time across

town, a farmer and his wife owned a/an _____ that laid

a _____ egg. They thought this would make them rich.

Each day, they sold the egg for things they wanted. They bought

_____ and _____ _____ for

their children. They bought _____ _____

for their house. It wasn't enough. So they cut open the egg-

laying beast to get all the riches at once. But all they found

were _____ filled with _____ .

HONK! Their greed had ruined everything.

Adverbs

An **adverb** is a word that tells more about a verb.
It can tell how, when, or where.

We yelled **loudly**.   (how)

We went to school **yesterday**.   (when)

We played **outside**.   (where)

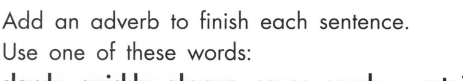

Add an adverb to finish each sentence.
Use one of these words:
slowly, **quickly**, **always**, **never**, **nearby**, **upstairs**.

The car moved _____ .

She _____ plays in the park.

Our grandmother lives _____ .

Sight Words

Say each word. Trace it. Say the letter names.

🍦	⚽	🍌	🦆
dentist	beetles	always	sleepy
teacher	pickles	loudly	giant
giraffe	teeth	sometimes	giggling
clown	hair	sadly	sour
penguin	tires	happily	scared

Questions and Answers

I am a curious kid with lots of questions. Yesterday, I asked

two questions to a _____ 🦆 _____ 🍦 .

Q: When do you normally eat breakfast?

A: Each morning, I _____ 🍌 munch on

_____ ⚽ and toast before sunrise.

Q: Where do you mostly live?

A: I _____ 🍌 live outside with my

best friend, a _____ 🍦 .

Hmmm. What should I ask next?

WRITING: Spelling and Grammar

Capitalize Holidays and Place Names

What begins with a capital letter?

- the name of a holiday
- the name of an exact place

We eat turkey on **Thanksgiving**.
My family moved to **New York**.

Fix each sentence.

I always give great gifts for christmas.

_____

The biggest state is alaska.

_____

Sight Words

Say each word. Trace it. Say the letter names.

year family ever

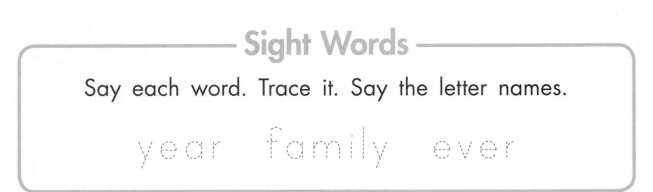

🥕	🦋	🍕
Broadway	Thanksgiving	Santa
Mars	Easter	George Washington
Timbuktu	Flag Day	Stinky
the North Pole	Groundhog Day	Goat

Christmas in New York City

Last year, my family went to _____ for _____ .
🥕 🦋

This year, my family is going to New York City for Christmas.

1. We will go to _____ to eat because it has the best
🥕

restaurants.

2. Then we will go to _____ to see a show. This year,
🥕

the stars of the show are a clown named _____ and a
🍕

snowman named _____ . They've been in this show since
🍕

_____ .
🦋

3. Finally, we will attend the holiday parade. We will

meet _____ . We'll tickle his beard, then
🍕

run away fast. This will be the best Christmas ever!

Commas in Letters and Greetings

Use a comma after the greeting and closing in a letter.

Dear Grandpa, **(greeting)**

We will come to visit you this summer.

I hope you have time to take us swimming.

We can't wait to see you!

Love, **(closing)**

Ben and Sophie

Add commas to the letter.

Dear Luis

I can't wait to send you the book I bought.

It is about dinosaurs. Your favorite!

Your friend

Paloma

Sight Words

Say each word. Trace it. Say the letter names.

been   talk   weren't

🐴	👕	🍍	🐟
Dear	best friend	giant	sleep
Yo	booger	purple	nibble
Hey hey	dear	hairless	complain
What's up	you	silver	juggle

The Letter

_____ _____ ,
🐴 👕

We need to talk. You won't believe what happened to me yesterday. My

friends and I went to the _____ park to _____ .
🍍 🐟

But instead, we saw a bunch of _____ aliens from
🍍

outer space. I swear! They had flown on their spaceships to Earth

to _____ . At least, that's what they said. They looked
🐟

like _____ men with _____ beards. We
🍍 🍍

weren't frightened, so we all decided to _____
🐟

until midnight. You should have been there!

Your _____ ,
👕

Me

WRITING: Spelling and Grammar

Possessives

A **possessive** noun shows who or what owns something.

Add **'s** to a noun that names one thing. (singular noun)

> This is the grizzly **bear's** cave.

Add just an **'** to a noun that names more than one thing, and ends in **s**. (plural noun)

> The three **boys'** rooms are filled with books.

If a plural noun does NOT end in **s**, add **'s**.

> The **men's** team rode the bus to the game.

Fix each sentence.

The scientists found a dinosaur___ bones.

All four dogs___ food was kept under the sink.

The women___ hats were on sale.

Sight Words

Say each word. Trace it. Say the letter names.

always   love   especially

🌶	❄	🧁
elephant	smelly	giggle
shark	hairy	dance
chicken	angry	juggle
sister	rubber	whistle

Our Pet

My pet _____ has many things! My pet's pet
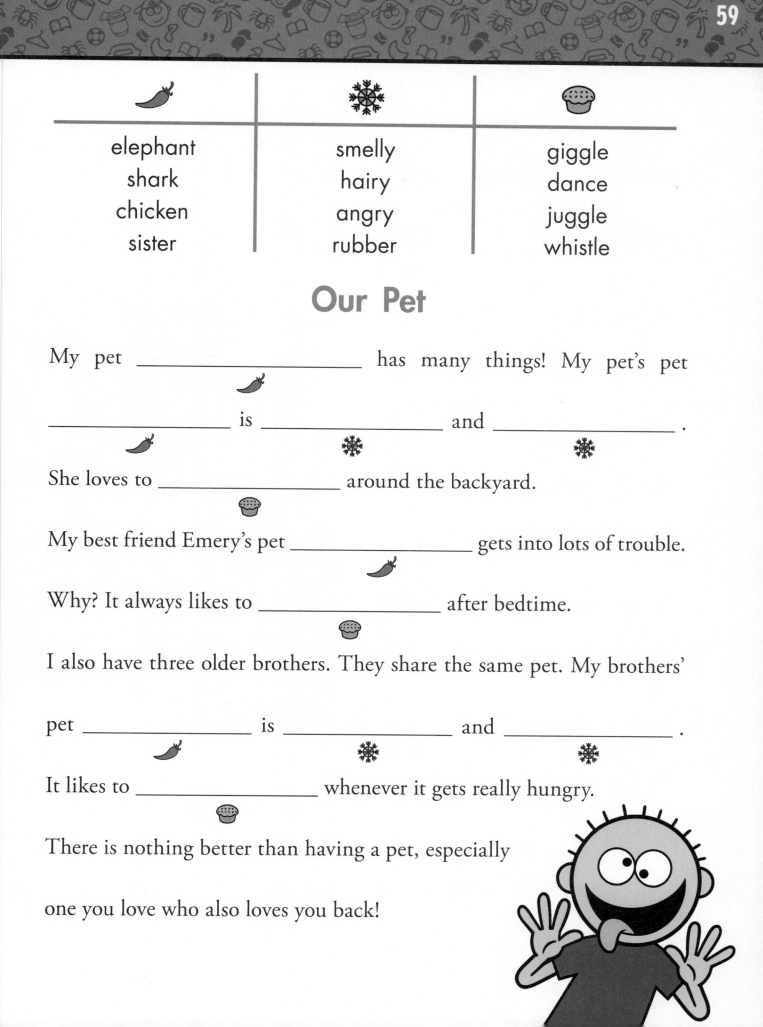

_____ is _____ and _____ .

She loves to _____ around the backyard.

My best friend Emery's pet _____ gets into lots of trouble.

Why? It always likes to _____ after bedtime.

I also have three older brothers. They share the same pet. My brothers'

pet _____ is _____ and _____ .

It likes to _____ whenever it gets really hungry.

There is nothing better than having a pet, especially

one you love who also loves you back!

WRITING: Spelling and Grammar

Complete Sentences

A **complete sentence** has a subject and a verb.

subject	verb
The children	laughed.
My mother	teaches.

Circle each complete sentence.

The bakery

My family flew to Florida.

The cows moo.

is running

Many people eat pizza.

— Sight Words —

Say each word. Trace it. Say the letter names.

these   upon   grandmother

🍌	🍅	🌴	🐳
forest	swimming	thorny	Burp
barn	dancing	sneezy	Stop
museum	skiing	fishy	Mommy
bathroom	tumbling	rotten	Noodles

Little Riding Hood

Once upon a time, Little _____ Riding Hood
(🌴)

was _____ through a _____ .
(🍅) (🍌)

She stumbled upon a _____ wolf who had eaten her
(🌴)

grandmother. " _____ !" said the wolf. "Follow me
(🐳)

to the _____ and we can go _____ ."
(🍌) (🍅)

" _____ !" said Little Riding Hood. "I need to deliver
(🐳)

these _____ cookies to my grandmother." "Give them
(🌴)

to me," yelled the wolf. " _____ !" said Little
(🐳)

Riding Hood, and she stood there watching the wolf

_____ away. That was the end of
(🍅)

the cookies. And that's the end of the tale.

Compound Sentences

A **compound sentence** has two sentences put together.
The words **and**, **but**, **or**, and **so** are used to
make a compound sentence.
A comma (,) is put before one of these words.

Mark played soccer, **and** I read a book.

I like to sleep late, **but** I have to get up early tomorrow.

Put together the two sentences to make a compound.

I play soccer.   My brother plays basketball.

_____

We like to eat candy.   Our school doesn't allow it.

_____

_____

Sight Words

Say each word. Trace it. Say the letter names.

after   money   wanted

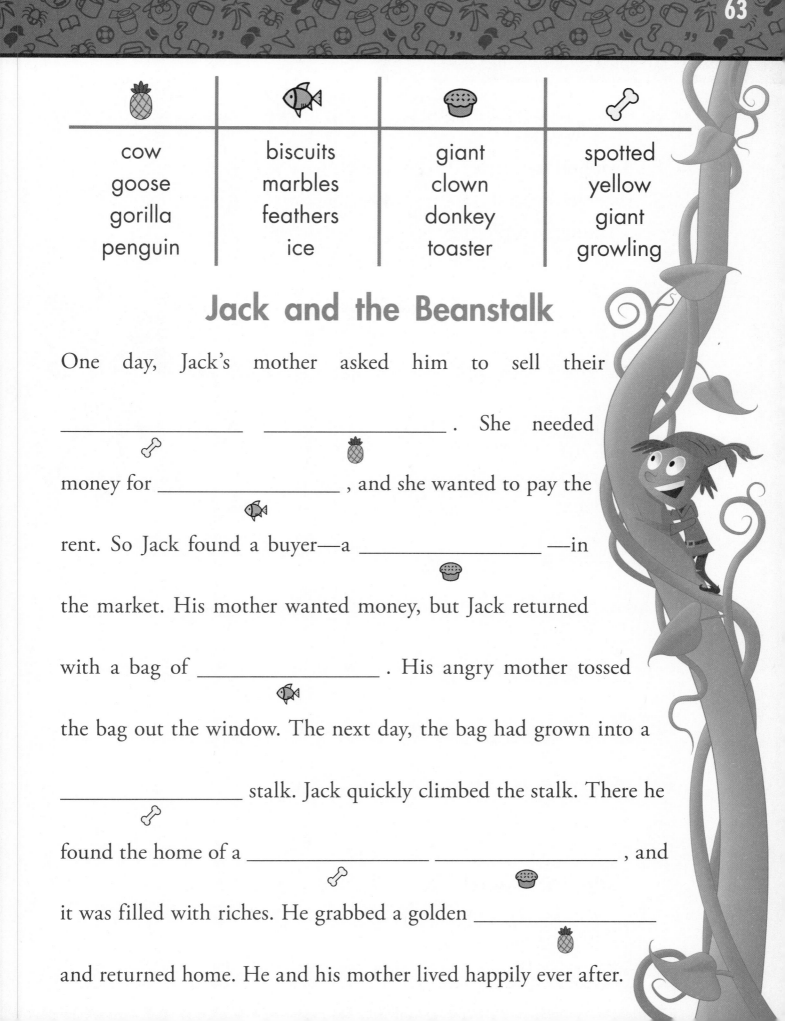			
cow	biscuits	giant	spotted
goose	marbles	clown	yellow
gorilla	feathers	donkey	giant
penguin	ice	toaster	growling

Jack and the Beanstalk

One day, Jack's mother asked him to sell their

_____ _____ . She needed

money for _____ , and she wanted to pay the

rent. So Jack found a buyer—a _____ —in

the market. His mother wanted money, but Jack returned

with a bag of _____ . His angry mother tossed

the bag out the window. The next day, the bag had grown into a

_____ stalk. Jack quickly climbed the stalk. There he

found the home of a _____ _____ , and

it was filled with riches. He grabbed a golden _____

and returned home. He and his mother lived happily ever after.

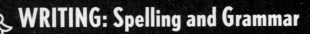

Contractions

A **contraction** is a shortened way to write two words. The letter or letters left out when putting together the two words are replaced by an apostrophe (').

I am = I'm   is not = isn't

I have = I've   he will = he'll

she is = she's   let us = let's

Write the contraction for each word pair.

are not _____   we will _____

we have _____   he is _____

does not _____   was not _____

she will _____   there is _____

Sight Words

Say each word. Trace it. Say the letter names.

could   should   tomorrow

🐶	⚽	❄️	🍕
circus	painted	brother	muddy
mall	cooked	doll	skinny
ocean	clapped	pooch	fuzzy
moon	raced	tiger	tiny
rodeo	giggled	buddy	broken

Could've, Would've, Should've

Some days it's difficult to decide what to do. Yesterday, I could've

gone to the _____ 🐶 , because it isn't very far away.

Instead, I _____ ⚽ with my _____ 🍕

_____ ❄️ all day long. Wasn't that better? Yesterday, I

would've _____ ⚽ with my _____ 🍕

_____ ❄️ . But it started to storm, and I didn't want to get wet.

Yesterday, I know I should've _____ ⚽ at home, but nope.

I went to the _____ 🐶 , where I _____ ⚽

all afternoon. I can't think of anything more fun.

Will I do these things tomorrow? Maybe.

Prefixes

A **prefix** is a word part added to the beginning of a word.
It changes the meaning of the word.

un = not, the opposite of

re = again

happy   **un**happy (not happy)

read   **re**read   (read again)

Add **un** or **re** to finish each word.

___tie   ___do

___make   ___able

___friendly ___appear

Sight Words

Say each word. Trace it. Say the letter names.

around away onto

🥕	🦔	🦴	🍍
unhappy	recycle	rabbit	plastic
unfriendly	refreeze	pickle	cotton
unhealthy	rebuild	booger	bacon
uncooked	rewash	lion	soupy
unsure	recook	tree	slippery

The Magic Act

It's time for an unreal and unbelievable magic act. The _____ 🥕

magician steps onto the stage. He's holding a _____ . 🦴

A gentle tap on his _____ hat and POOF! It is gone. 🍍

The crowd gasps. Then another tap and POOF! It reappears. The

crowd claps in amazement. What could be next? The magician unties

his _____ cape and waves it around. 🍍

This time, he will try to _____ a 🦔

_____ . Abracadabra! But no, the 🦴

magician is unlucky. He rewraps the cape around

his neck, then slips away as the crowd boos.

VOCABULARY

Prefixes

A **prefix** is a word part added to the beginning of a word. It changes the meaning of the word.

dis =   not, the opposite of

mis = bad, wrong, incorrectly

like   **dis**like   (the opposite of like)

treat   **mis**treat   (treat badly or wrongly)

Add **dis** or **mis** to finish each word.

_____agree   _____use

_____obey   _____able

_____understood   _____appear

Sight Words

Say each word. Trace it. Say the letter names.

never   problem   hour

🐟	🍉	👕	🦢
rabbit	disappoint	baby	Poodles
hippo	disturb	sailboat	Puddles
sausage	distract	mommy	Bubbles
flower	misread	tomato	Stinky
pigeon	mistake	pencil	Bob

Back and Forth

One day, I saw a _____ and a _____
🐟   🐟

argue. They were having a terrible disagreement. One said, "You

should never disobey a _____ if it's really happy. You
👕

should also never _____ or misname your pet."
🍉

The other said, "It's not a big problem if you misname your pet

_____ or _____ . You should also never
🦢   🦢

disobey a _____ if it's really angry."
👕

Back and forth they fought. I listened for almost an

hour. But I dislike fighting, so what did I do?

I disappeared.

VOCABULARY

Suffixes

A **suffix** is a word part added to the end of a word. It changes the meaning of the word.

ful = full of, with

less = without, not

fear   fear**ful**   (full of fear)

hope   hope**less**   (without hope)

Add **ful** or **less** to finish each word.

care_____   weight_____

harm_____   color_____

pain_____   joy_____

Sight Words

Say each word. Trace it. Say the letter names.

school   few   beautiful

crocodile	dragon	sings	belly
ghost	goblin	sleeps	eyebrow
president	tree	sneezes	slipper
cookie	carrot	barfs	mother

The Interview

For school, I have to interview a _____ or a

_____ . Here are a few of my questions.

1. Do you feel fearful when a _____ _____ ?

2. Is it useless or useful to have a _____ that

_____ ?

3. Do you think it's painful for a _____ to tickle your

_____ ?

4. Which is more beautiful—a purple _____

or a hairy _____ ?

So, what do you think? What other questions should I ask?

VOCABULARY

Suffixes

A **suffix** is a word part added to the end of a word. It changes the meaning of the word.

ly = in a certain way

y = full of

slow   slow**ly**   (in a slow way)

rain   rain**y**   (full of rain)

Add **ly** or **y** to finish each word.

itch _____   calm ___

eager ___   grass ___

year ____   need ___

--- Sight Words ---

Say each word. Trace it. Say the letter names.

their   great   of

🦋	🦴	🏀	🍌
turtle	fluffy	quickly	danced
skunk	itchy	slowly	wiggled
whale	toothy	quietly	flipped
giraffe	kooky	loudly	flew
witch	bloody	proudly	drove

Driving Through Africa

My family took their yearly trip to the _____
🦴

plains of Africa. We grabbed our cameras. Why? We spotted a/an

_____ _____ in a tree. Snap! What a great
🦴 🦋

selfie! Just then, a zebra _____ _____ by,
🏀 🍌

and we raced to take a photo. After that, our _____ guide
🦴

gave us lunch. As we ate, a herd of elephants _____ past
🍌

our picnic table. It was quite a sight! We stayed and

watched the hyenas as they _____
🏀

_____ away until sunset.
🍌

I wonder what we'll see next year!

VOCABULARY

Compound Words

Compound words are two or more words that together make a new word.

Often the meanings of the smaller words can help you figure out the meaning of the longer word.

bed + room = bedroom

snow + flake = snowflake

Write the compound word.

Draw a picture of one of the words.

rain + coat _____

pop + corn _____

basket + ball _____

butter + fly _____

— Sight Words —

Say each word. Trace it. Say the letter names.

which anywhere goes

🐶	🐟	🧁
birdbath	snowflake	sunflower
dollhouse	doorknob	toothbrush
doghouse	starfish	rainbow
spaceship	peanut	jellyfish
supermarket	dragonfly	cowboy

Snowballs vs. Sunshine

Which season is your favorite? My brother and I disagree. I like the

snow, so winter is my favorite. In winter, I like to go to a

_____ and play with my _____ . Anywhere
🐶 🐟

I can find a _____ and a _____ can
🐟 🐟

be fun! Other kids put on their snowsuits and build snowmen.

My brother likes the sunshine. So summer is his favorite. He likes

to go to a _____ at the beach. He goes with his favorite
🐶

_____ . Someplace that has a _____ and a
🧁 🧁

_____ is perfect for him. Other kids play baseball and
🧁

make hot dogs at cookouts. Which season is your favorite?

VOCABULARY

Shades of Meaning: Verbs

Verbs are action words. Some verbs mean almost the same thing. However, each verb has a slightly different meaning.

whisper   (talk quietly)
talk   (talk normally)
babble   (talk without making sense)

Add a verb to finish each sentence: **ate, nibbled, devoured.**

I _____ my dinner. It was very tasty.

I _____ the sandwich. I was starving!

I _____ on a cracker. I wasn't very hungry.

Sight Words

Say each word. Trace it. Say the letter names.

long   group   very

�- (ball)	🦴 (bone)	🍉 (watermelon)	🐋 (whale)
clowns	munching	chatting	turnips
sharks	slurping	gossiping	snakes
penguins	burping	whispering	worms
sailors	nibbling	shouting	boogers

The Restaurant

My family went on a long trip. Along the way, we stopped at many

restaurants. But this was the weirdest! Sitting at one table was a group

of _____ (ball). They were _____ (bone) on boiled

_____ (whale). Beside them was a table of _____ (ball).

They were _____ (bone) on barbecue _____ (whale).

It looked very tasty! At the counter sat three _____ (ball).

They were _____ (bone) on pickled _____ (whale) and

_____ (watermelon) about their vacation. My family sat at the only

empty table. We took one look at the menu.

And what did we do? We ordered one of

everything, of course!

Shades of Meaning: Verbs

Verbs are action words. Some verbs mean almost the same thing. However, each verb has a slightly different meaning.

walk   run   march

Add a verb to finish each sentence: **looked, stared, glanced**.

I _____ at that boy until he stopped talking.

I _____ at the paper, but I don't know what it said.

I _____ at the beach. It was full of people.

Sight Words

Say each word. Trace it. Say the letter names.

stood   so   baby

🍌	👕	🍅
baby	marched	feathered
turtle	pranced	silver
dinosaur	twirled	three-legged
flea	flapped	grouchy

The Race

Today was the day of the biggest race in the county! All the racers

lined up at the starting line. There stood a _____

_____ , a _____ 🍅 _____ , and a

🍌 _____ 🍅 _____ . The announcer shouted, "On

🍅 🍌

your mark. Get set. Go!" The racers _____ through the

👕

park, but one racer stopped to take a nap. Then they _____

👕

around the lake, but one racer stopped to take a bath. Finally, they

_____ onto the bridge, but one racer fell over it. So who

👕

was the winner? A _____ _____ appeared from

🍅 🍌

the crowd and crossed the finish line. And no one cared.

FINISH

Shades of Meaning: Adjectives

Adjectives are describing words. Some adjectives mean almost the same thing. However, each adjective has a slightly different meaning.

large   (big)
huge   (very big)
gigantic   (very, very big)

Add an adjective to finish each sentence: **small**, **tiny**.

I see a _____ baby. She is so cute!

Can you find the _____ bead? It fell off my necklace.

Sight Words

Say each word. Trace it. Say the letter names.

ago   house   together

❄	🐚	🍧	🍅
goose	little	large	Baby
whale	mini	enormous	Beast
mosquito	teeny	gigantic	Sweetie
yak	wee	hulking	Pickles

The Pet

Long ago, an older lady named Mildred lived in my

neighborhood. She had a house filled with pets. Everyone

around liked to visit to play with them. Especially me!

Mildred had a/an _____ pet _____ named
   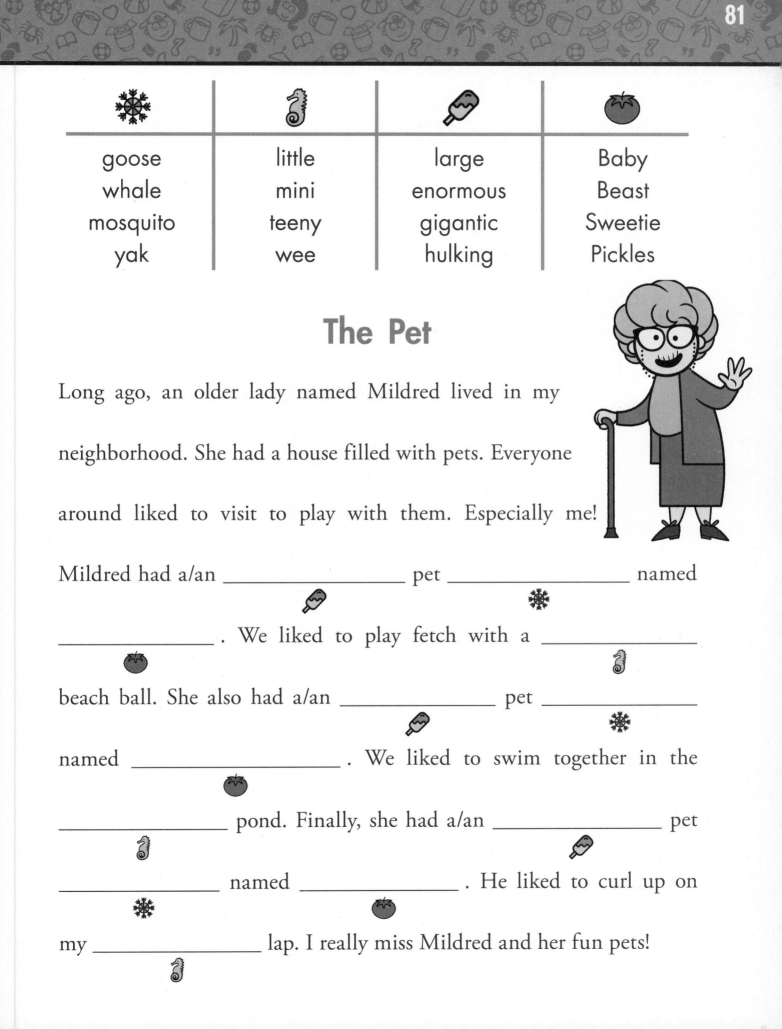 🍧   ❄

_____ . We liked to play fetch with a _____
   🍅   🐚

beach ball. She also had a/an _____ pet _____
                                    🍧   ❄

named _____ . We liked to swim together in the
          🍅

_____ pond. Finally, she had a/an _____ pet
   🐚   🍧

_____ named _____ . He liked to curl up on
   ❄   🍅

my _____ lap. I really miss Mildred and her fun pets!
      🐚

VOCABULARY

Shades of Meaning: Adjectives

Adjectives are describing words. Some adjectives mean almost the same thing. However, each adjective has a slightly different meaning.

chilly (a little cold)
cold
freezing (very cold)

Add an adjective to finish each sentence: **pretty, beautiful**.

That is the most _____ sunset in the world!

The sunrise is _____.

Sight Words

Say each word. Trace it. Say the letter names.

twice   leave   drink

🥕	🐋	🦔	🌴
squirrels	steamy	shivering	swimsuit
penguins	scorching	icy	towel
pigeons	blazing	frozen	shoe
seals	flaring	polar	skirt

Santa Is Coming

In my town, Santa comes twice a year. In December, Santa rides in on

his _____ sleigh pulled by six _____ reindeer.
        🦔   🦔

He wears a/an _____ red hat and _____ .
                    🦔   🌴

Through the whipping winds, you can hear his hearty "Ho, ho, ho!"

I always leave cookies for him to eat. But in July, Santa comes in

on his _____ sleigh, pulled by six _____
            🐋   🐋

_____ . He wears a tiny _____ and
      🥕   🌴

_____ . Through the light breeze, you can hear his soft
      🌴

"Ho, ho, hot!" So I always leave water for him to

drink. I love that Santa comes twice a year!

VOCABULARY

Character

A **character** is who a story is about.

Sam   dog   Cinderella

Write the names of three characters you like.

1. _____

2. _____

3. _____

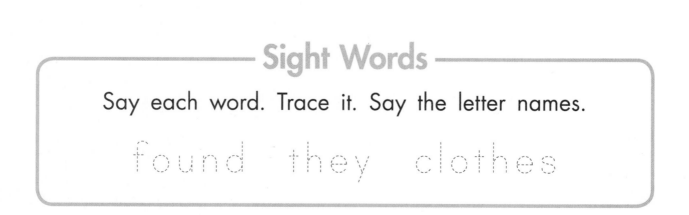

Sight Words

Say each word. Trace it. Say the letter names.

found   they   clothes

 🐟	❄️	🧁	🐶
frog	dragons	washed	hairy
witch	elves	pickled	handsome
buffalo	senators	trashed	shy
dancer	dolls	ripped	scaly

Snow White

Once upon a time, a _____

🐶

_____ named Snow White

🐟

lived in the forest. The evil queen hated Snow

White. Why? Because the queen wanted to be the most beautiful

in the land. So Snow White ran deeper into the forest to hide. She

found the hut where seven _____ lived. They hid Snow

❄️

White. To thank them, Snow White _____ their food.

🧁

She _____ their clothes and _____ their

🧁 🧁

house, too. One day a _____ prince showed up. "I will

🐶

save you," he said. "No thanks," said Snow White. "I can save myself."

And she lived happily ever after.

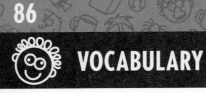

VOCABULARY

Setting

The **setting** is where and when a story takes place.

home

beach

Write the names of three settings you know.

1. _____

2. _____

3. _____

— Sight Words —

Say each word. Trace it. Say the letter names.

before   eight   super

🍕	🦴	🌶️	🏀
park	giant	horses	skinny
ocean	fly	TVs	hairy
mall	clown	apples	spooky
zoo	unicorn	butts	talking

Lost

One day, my sister and I got lost in the _____ 🍕 . I mean,

super lost! First, we stumbled upon a little _____ 🍕 where

a giant _____ 🦴 lived. I screamed, and my sister wet her

pants. So we ran until we came to a crowded _____ 🍕 .

There, about a hundred _____ 🌶️ came flying at us. We

hid behind two _____ 🏀 trees. Finally, we ended up at

a/an _____ 🍕 . A _____ 🦴 came over and said,

"Hello!" Then it turned into eight _____ 🌶️ . Yowza! I don't

know how, but after that we found our way home.

And that is where we will stay from now on!

Plot

The **plot** includes the main things that happen in a story. A story plot has a beginning, a middle, and an end.

>**Beginning**: A girl loses her cat.
>**Middle**: A girl looks for her cat.
>**End**: A girl finds her cat.

Write the plot of a story you know.

Beginning: _____

_____

Middle: _____

_____

End: _____

_____

——— Sight Words ———

Say each word. Trace it. Say the letter names.

🥕	🦋	🍌	🦔
Runaway	danced	slithered	itchy
Stinky	wiggled	bounced	golden
Mister	sneezed	flew	grassy
Tutu	farted	skipped	busy

Gingerbread Man

Once upon a time, an old woman made a man out of gingerbread. He

hopped out of the oven and _____ away. So everyone
🦋

called him the _____ Man. He _____
🥕   🦋

past the barn and _____ through the city. Then,
🦋

he _____ over the mountains until he reached the
🍌

river. Once at the river, he spotted a hungry crocodile. "Hop on my

_____ back," said the crocodile. "I will take you far away."
🦔

So the man _____ on the crocodile.
🍌

SNAP! The crocodile took him far away,

indeed. Straight to his belly! THE END

VOCABULARY

Main Ideas

The **main ideas** are the most important facts in a text.

Book Title: Sharks
1. Live in the ocean.
2. Have sharp teeth.
3. Breathe through gills.

Read the main ideas. Write a title for this book.

Book Title: _____
1. It has a big red barn.
2. Animals, like horses and cows, live there.
3. Farmers grow crops, like corn, there.

―――― Sight Words ――――

Say each word. Trace it. Say the letter names.

really   common   interesting

Tasks

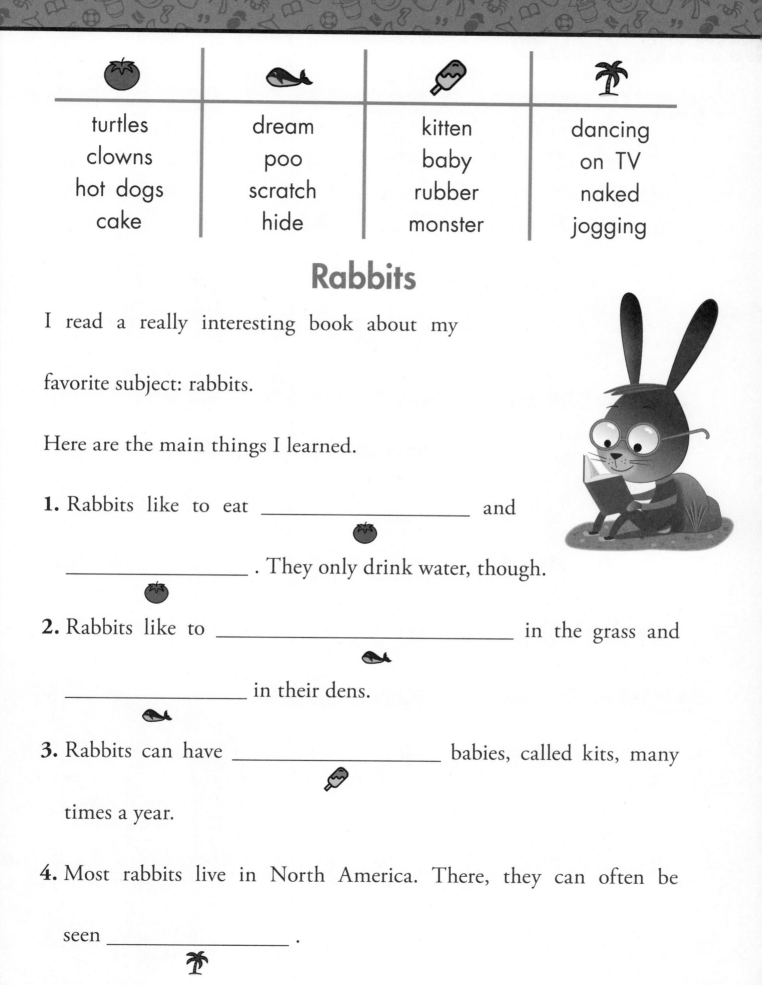

ANSWER KEY

6 · PHONICS

Short Vowels

Short vowels can be spelled many ways.

bl**a**ck   sh**i**p   fr**o**g

dr**u**m   sl**e**d   h**ea**d

Add a short vowel spelling to finish each picture name.

s **o** cks   tr **u** ck   br **ea** d

l **a** mp   p **u** mpk **i** n   k **i** tt **e** n

— Sight Words —
Say each word. Trace it. Say the letter names.

who there friend

8 · PHONICS

Blends

When two consonants are together in a word, we often hear the sound of both letters.

flower   **st**op   **pr**incess

Add two letters to finish each picture name.

g r een   **p l** ane   **s k** unk

s p in   **d r** agon   **s m** elling

— Sight Words —
Say each word. Trace it. Say the letter names.

over lived already

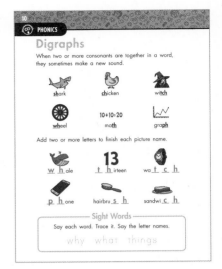

10 · PHONICS

Digraphs

When two or more consonants are together in a word, they sometimes make a new sound.

s**h**ark   **ch**icken   wit**ch**

wheel   math   grap**h**

Add two or more letters to finish each picture name.

w h ale   **t h** irteen   wa **t c h**

p h one   hairbru **s h**   sandwi **c h**

— Sight Words —
Say each word. Trace it. Say the letter names.

why what things

12 · PHONICS

Final e

When a word ends in **e**, the vowel before it and the **e** work together to say the vowel's name.

kit   kit**e**

Add a vowel (a, e, i, o, u) and e (at the end) to finish each picture name.

sk **a** t **e**   n **i** n **e**   r **o** s **e**

c **u** b **e**   gr **a** p **e** s   c **a** k **e**

— Sight Words —
Say each word. Trace it. Say the letter names.

you some maybe

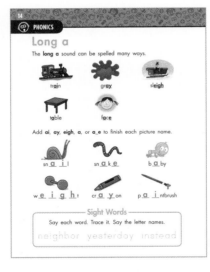

14 · PHONICS

Long a

The **long a** sound can be spelled many ways.

tr**ai**n   gr**ay**   sl**eigh**

t**a**ble   f**a**ce

Add ai, ay, eigh, a, or a_e to finish each picture name.

sn **ai** l   sn **a** k **e**   b **a** by

w **ei** gh t   cr **a y** on   p **ai** ntbrush

— Sight Words —
Say each word. Trace it. Say the letter names.

neighbor yesterday instead

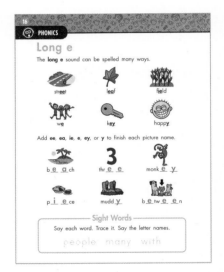

16 · PHONICS

Long e

The **long e** sound can be spelled many ways.

str**ee**t   l**ea**f   fi**e**ld

w**e**   k**ey**   happ**y**

Add ee, ea, ie, e, ey, or y to finish each picture name.

b **ea** ch   thr **e e**   monk **e y**

p **i e** ce   mudd **y**   b **e** tw **ee** n

— Sight Words —
Say each word. Trace it. Say the letter names.

people many with

18 · PHONICS

Long o

The **long o** sound can be spelled many ways.

g**oa**t   sn**ow**man   r**o**pe

g**o**   t**oe**s

Add oa, ow, o_e, o, or oe to finish each picture name.

st **o** n **e** s   gh **o** st   thr **o a** t

rainb **o w**   tic-tac-t **o e**   buffal **o**

— Sight Words —
Say each word. Trace it. Say the letter names.

our too doesn't

20 · PHONICS

Long i

The **long i** sound can be spelled many ways.

br**igh**t   t**ie**   cr**y**

k**i**te   ch**i**ld

Add igh, ie, y, i_e, or i to finish each picture name.

p **ie** s   n **igh** t   butterfl **y**

s **i** d **e** walk   f **i** nd

— Sight Words —
Say each word. Trace it. Say the letter names.

would should through

22 PHONICS

Long u

The **long u** sound can be spelled many ways.

f**ew**

m**u**sic

m**u**le

arg**ue**

Add **ew**, **u**, **u_e**, or **ue** to finish each picture name.

c**u**b**e**

f**e**w

resc**ue**

men**u**

— Sight Words —
Say each word. Trace it. Say the letter names.

most won't another

24 PHONICS

r-Controlled Vowels
er, ir, ur

The letters **er**, **ir**, and **ur** all stand for the same sounds.

shirt

turtle

fern

Add **er**, **ir**, or **ur** to finish each picture name.

sk**ir**t

f**ir**st

p**ur**ple

moth**er**

— Sight Words —
Say each word. Trace it. Say the letter names.

I'd wouldn't because

26 PHONICS

r-Controlled Vowels
or, ore, ar

When a vowel is followed by the letter **r**, the **r** affects the vowel sound. It is neither long nor short.

corn

car

The "or" sounds can also be spelled **ore** as in **more** and **oar** as in **roaring**.

Add **or** or **ar** to finish each picture name.

b**ar**n

h**or**n

f**or**k

st**ar**s

f**ar**mer

thunderst**or**m

— Sight Words —
Say each word. Trace it. Say the letter names.

do more put

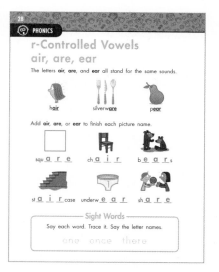

28 PHONICS

r-Controlled Vowels
air, are, ear

The letters **air**, **are**, and **ear** all stand for the same sounds.

h**air**

silverw**are**

p**ear**

Add **air**, **are**, or **ear** to finish each picture name.

squ**are**

ch**air**

b**ear**s

st**air**case

underw**ear**

sh**are**

— Sight Words —
Say each word. Trace it. Say the letter names.

one once there

30 PHONICS

Diphthongs oi, oy; ou, ow

Some vowel sounds feel like they move around in your mouth.

cowb**oy**

b**oi**l

m**ou**th

cl**ow**n

Add **oy**, **oi**, **ou**, or **ow** to finish each picture name.

s**oi**l

dogh**ou**se

t**oy**s

br**ow**n

cr**ow**n

c**oi**ns

— Sight Words —
Say each word. Trace it. Say the letter names.

girls come might

---

32 PHONICS

Variant Vowels oo

The letters **oo** stand for two different sounds. These sounds can be spelled many ways.

f**oo**t

m**oo**n

bl**ue**

gr**ou**p

n**ew**

J**u**ne

The "oo" sounds can also be spelled **ould** as in **could** and **u** as in **put**.

Add **oo**, **ue**, or **ou** to finish each picture name.

b**oo**kcase

sp**oo**n

mushr**oo**m

gl**ue**

s**ou**p

c**oo**king

— Sight Words —
Say each word. Trace it. Say the letter names.

before your special

34 PHONICS

Variant Vowels
au, aw, augh, ough, al

The vowel sound in **all** can be spelled many ways.

dr**aw**

s**au**sage

f**all**

t**al**k

s**al**t

The "aw" sounds can also be spelled **ough** as in **bought** and **augh** as in **taught**.

Add **aw**, **au**, or **al** to finish each picture name.

sidew**al**k

cr**aw**ling

baseb**al**l

l**au**nching

— Sight Words —
Say each word. Trace it. Say the letter names.

friend everyone probably

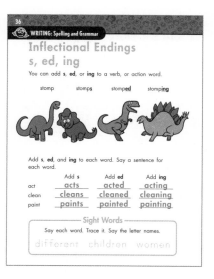

36 WRITING: Spelling and Grammar

Inflectional Endings
s, ed, ing

You can add **s**, **ed**, or **ing** to a verb, or action word.

stomp   stomp**s**   stomp**ed**   stomp**ing**

Add **s**, **ed**, and **ing** to each word. Say a sentence for each word.

	Add s	Add ed	Add ing
act	acts	acted	acting
clean	cleans	cleaned	cleaning
paint	paints	painted	painting

— Sight Words —
Say each word. Trace it. Say the letter names.

different children women

---

38 WRITING: Spelling and Grammar

Inflectional Endings with Spelling Changes

When you add **s**, **es**, **ed**, or **ing** to a word, you sometimes have to change the spelling before adding the ending.

1. Double the final consonant
stop   stops   sto**pp**ed   sto**pp**ing

2. Drop e
save   saves   saved   saving

3. Change y to i
cry   cr**i**es   cr**i**ed   crying

Add **s**, **ed**, and **ing** to each word.

	Add s or es	Add ed	Add ing
tap	taps	tapped	tapping
bake	bakes	baked	baking
try	tries	tried	trying

— Sight Words —
Say each word. Trace it. Say the letter names.

brother my something

ANSWER KEY

---

40 WRITING: Spelling and Grammar

Irregular Plural Nouns

A **plural** word is more than one of something.
Most naming words, or nouns, add **s** or **es** to make it plural.
However, some plural words do not. We call them irregular.

Regular

1 cat   2 cat**s**
1 box   2 box**es**

Irregular

1 man   2 men
1 mouse 2 mice

Write the plural of each word.

1 foot   2 __feet__   1 woman   2 __women__
1 knife   2 __knives__   1 child   2 __children__
1 tooth   2 __teeth__   1 sheep   2 __sheep__

— Sight Words —
Say each word. Trace it. Say the letter names.
been   long   pictures

---

42 WRITING: Spelling and Grammar

Collective Nouns

A **collective noun** is used to name a group of people,
animals, or things.

A <u>crowd</u> of people   A <u>crew</u> of sailors
A <u>herd</u> of cows   A <u>flock</u> of geese
A <u>stack</u> of books   A <u>heap</u> of trash

Add a collective noun to finish each picture name.
Use **batch, herd, set,** or **class.**

A __herd__ of elephants

A __set__ of bowls

A __batch__ of cookies

A __class__ of students

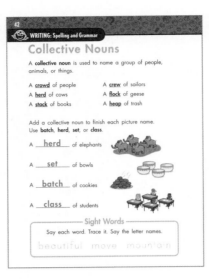

— Sight Words —
Say each word. Trace it. Say the letter names.
beautiful   move   mountain

---

44 WRITING: Spelling and Grammar

Reflexive Pronouns

Reflexive pronouns are words ending in **self** or **selves.**

myself   yourself   himself
herself   oneself   itself
ourselves   yourselves   themselves

Use a word from above to finish each sentence.

He helped __himself__ to a big bowl of soup.

We saved __ourselves__ from doing all that work.

I looked at __myself__ in the bathroom mirror.

They bought __themselves__ new uniforms for
the big game.

— Sight Words —
Say each word. Trace it. Say the letter names.
caught   sure   today

---

46 WRITING: Spelling and Grammar

Verbs

Verbs are action words.
Present tense verbs tell about things
happening now. Past tense verbs tell
about things that already happened.

Today, I **paint** my house. (present)
Yesterday, I **painted** my friend's house. (past)

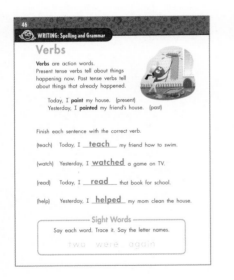

Finish each sentence with the correct verb.

(teach)   Today, I __teach__ my friend how to swim.

(watch)   Yesterday, I __watched__ a game on TV.

(read)   Today, I __read__ that book for school.

(help)   Yesterday, I __helped__ my mom clean the house.

— Sight Words —
Say each word. Trace it. Say the letter names.
two   were   again

---

48 WRITING: Spelling and Grammar

Irregular Past-Tense Verbs

Most past tense verbs end in **ed.**
Today, I **walk** to the store. (present)
Yesterday, I **walked** to the store. (past)

However, some verbs do not.
We call these irregular.
Today, I **run** in the park. (present)
Yesterday, I **ran** in the park. (past)

Finish each sentence with the past tense form of each verb.

(bite)   Yesterday, I __bit__ into the apple.

(send)   Yesterday, I __sent__ an e-mail to my friend.

(buy)   Yesterday, I __bought__ a new soccer ball.

(drink)   Yesterday, I __drank__ a big glass of milk.

— Sight Words —
Say each word. Trace it. Say the letter names.
thought   taught   possible

---

50 WRITING: Spelling and Grammar

Adjectives

An **adjective** is a describing word.
It tells more about something.

a cat   a <u>little</u> cat   a <u>black</u> cat

Add adjectives to finish each sentence.
Answers will vary.
The _____ dog barks.

The dress is _____ .

The _____ boy has a _____ coat.

— Sight Words —
Say each word. Trace it. Say the letter names.
across   bought   enough

---

52 WRITING: Spelling and Grammar

Adverbs

An **adverb** is a word that tells more about a verb.
It can tell how, when, or where.

We yelled <u>loudly</u>.   (how)

We went to school <u>yesterday</u>. (when)

We played <u>outside</u>.   (where)

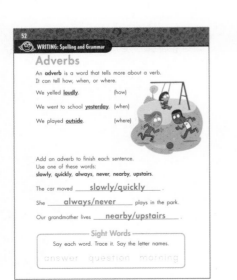

Add an adverb to finish each sentence.
Use one of these words:
slowly, quickly, always, never, nearby, upstairs.

The car moved __slowly/quickly__ .

She __always/never__ plays in the park.

Our grandmother lives __nearby/upstairs__ .

— Sight Words —
Say each word. Trace it. Say the letter names.
answer   question   morning

---

54 WRITING: Spelling and Grammar

Capitalize Holidays and Place Names

What begins with a capital letter?
• the name of a holiday
• the name of an exact place

We eat turkey on <u>Thanksgiving</u>.
My family moved to <u>New York</u>.

Fix each sentence.

I always give great gifts for christmas.
__I always give great gifts for Christmas.__

The biggest state is alaska.
__The biggest state is Alaska.__

— Sight Words —
Say each word. Trace it. Say the letter names.
year   family   ever

---

56 WRITING: Spelling and Grammar

Commas in Letters and Greetings

Use a comma after the greeting and closing in a letter.

Dear Grandpa, **(greeting)**
We will come to visit you this summer.
I hope you have time to take us swimming.
We can't wait to see you!
    Love, **(closing)**
    Ben and Sophie

Add commas to the letter.

Dear Luis **,**
I can't wait to send you the book I bought.
It is about dinosaurs. Your favorite!
    Your friend **,**
    Paloma

— Sight Words —
Say each word. Trace it. Say the letter names.
been   talk   weren't

58 WRITING: Spelling and Grammar

Possessives

A **possessive** noun shows who or what owns something.

Add **'s** to a noun that names one thing. (singular noun)

This is the grizzly **bear's** cave.

Add just an **'** to a noun that names more than one thing, and ends in **s**. (plural noun)

The three **boys'** rooms are filled with books.

If a plural noun does NOT end in **s**, add **'s**.

The **men's** team rode the bus to the game.

Fix each sentence.

The scientists found a dinosaur **'s** bones.

All four dogs **'** food was kept under the sink.

The women **'s** hats were on sale.

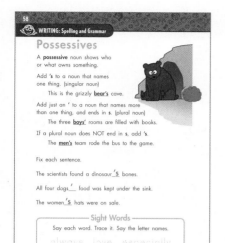

— Sight Words —
Say each word. Trace it. Say the letter names.

always love especially

60 WRITING: Spelling and Grammar

Complete Sentences

A **complete sentence** has a subject and a verb.

subject	verb
The children	laughed.
My mother	teaches.

Circle each complete sentence.

The bakery

(My family flew to Florida.)

(The cows moo.)

is running

(Many people eat pizza.)

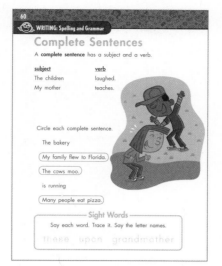

— Sight Words —
Say each word. Trace it. Say the letter names.

these upon grandmother

62 WRITING: Spelling and Grammar

Compound Sentences

A **compound sentence** has two sentences put together. The words **and, but, or,** and **so** are used to make a compound sentence.
A comma (**,**) is put before one of these words.

Mark played soccer**, and** I read a book.
I like to sleep late**, but** I have to get up early tomorrow.

Put together the two sentences to make a compound.

I play soccer.   My brother plays basketball.
I play soccer, and my brother plays basketball.

We like to eat candy.   Our school doesn't allow it.
We like to eat candy, but our school doesn't
allow it.

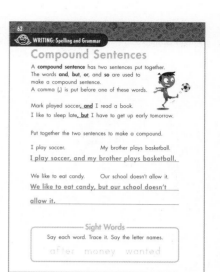

— Sight Words —
Say each word. Trace it. Say the letter names.

after money wanted

64 WRITING: Spelling and Grammar

Contractions

A **contraction** is a shortened way to write two words. The letter or letters left out when putting together the two words are replaced by an apostrophe (**'**).

I am = I'm	is not = isn't
I have = I've	he will = he'll
she is = she's	let us = let's

Write the contraction for each word pair.

are not	**aren't**	we will	**we'll**
we have	**we've**	he is	**he's**
does not	**doesn't**	was not	**wasn't**
she will	**she'll**	there is	**there's**

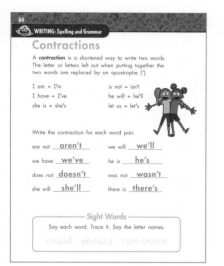

— Sight Words —
Say each word. Trace it. Say the letter names.

could should tomorrow

66 VOCABULARY

Prefixes

A **prefix** is a word part added to the beginning of a word. It changes the meaning of the word.

un = not, the opposite of
re = again

happy	**un**happy	(not happy)
read	**re**read	(read again)

Add **un** or **re** to finish each word.

un/retie   **un/re**do
un/remake   **un**able
unfriendly   **re**appear

POOF!

— Sight Words —
Say each word. Trace it. Say the letter names.

around away onto

68 VOCABULARY

Prefixes

A **prefix** is a word part added to the beginning of a word. It changes the meaning of the word.

dis = not, the opposite of
mis = bad, wrong, incorrectly

like	**dis**like	(the opposite of like)
treat	**mis**treat	(treat badly or wrongly)

Add **dis** or **mis** to finish each word.

disagree   **mis**use
disobey   **dis**able
misunderstood   **dis**appear

— Sight Words —
Say each word. Trace it. Say the letter names.

never problem hour

70 VOCABULARY

Suffixes

A **suffix** is a word part added to the end of a word. It changes the meaning of the word.

ful = full of, with
less = without, not

fear	fear**ful**	(full of fear)
hope	hope**less**	(without hope)

Add **ful** or **less** to finish each word.

care **ful/less**	weight **less**
harm **ful/less**	color **ful/less**
pain **ful/less**	joy **ful/less**

— Sight Words —
Say each word. Trace it. Say the letter names.

school few beautiful

72 VOCABULARY

Suffixes

A **suffix** is a word part added to the end of a word. It changes the meaning of the word.

ly = in a certain way
y = full of

slow	slow**ly**	(in a slow way)
rain	rain**y**	(full of rain)

Add **ly** or **y** to finish each word.

itch **y**	calm **ly**
eager **ly**	grass **y**
year **ly**	need **y**

— Sight Words —
Say each word. Trace it. Say the letter names.

their great of

74 VOCABULARY

Compound Words

Compound words are two or more words that together make a new word.
Often the meanings of the smaller words can help you figure out the meaning of the longer word.

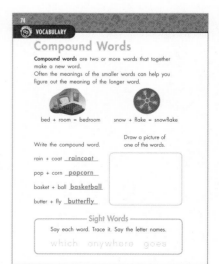

bed + room = bedroom   snow + flake = snowflake

Write the compound word.   Draw a picture of one of the words.

rain + coat   **raincoat**
pop + corn   **popcorn**
basket + ball   **basketball**
butter + fly   **butterfly**

— Sight Words —
Say each word. Trace it. Say the letter names.

which anywhere goes

ANSWER KEY

---

76 **VOCABULARY**

Shades of Meaning: Verbs

Verbs are action words. Some verbs mean almost the same thing. However, each verb has a slightly different meaning.

whisper (talk quietly)
talk (talk normally)
babble (talk without making sense)

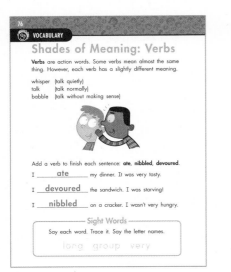

Add a verb to finish each sentence: **ate, nibbled, devoured**.

I ___**ate**___ my dinner. It was very tasty.

I ___**devoured**___ the sandwich. I was starving!

I ___**nibbled**___ on a cracker. I wasn't very hungry.

— Sight Words —
Say each word. Trace it. Say the letter names.

long   group   very

---

78 **VOCABULARY**

Shades of Meaning: Verbs

Verbs are action words. Some verbs mean almost the same thing. However, each verb has a slightly different meaning.

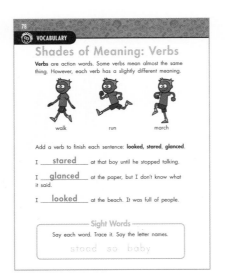

walk   run   march

Add a verb to finish each sentence: **looked, stared, glanced**.

I ___**stared**___ at that boy until he stopped talking.

I ___**glanced**___ at the paper, but I don't know what it said.

I ___**looked**___ at the beach. It was full of people.

— Sight Words —
Say each word. Trace it. Say the letter names.

stood   so   baby

---

80 **VOCABULARY**

Shades of Meaning: Adjectives

Adjectives are describing words. Some adjectives mean almost the same thing. However, each adjective has a slightly different meaning.

large (big)
huge (very big)
gigantic (very, very big)

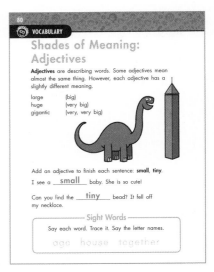

Add an adjective to finish each sentence: **small, tiny**.

I see a ___**small**___ baby. She is so cute!

Can you find the ___**tiny**___ bead? It fell off my necklace.

— Sight Words —
Say each word. Trace it. Say the letter names.

ago   house   together

---

82 **VOCABULARY**

Shades of Meaning: Adjectives

Adjectives are describing words. Some adjectives mean almost the same thing. However, each adjective has a slightly different meaning.

chilly (a little cold)
cold
freezing (very cold)

Add an adjective to finish each sentence: **pretty, beautiful**.

That is the most ___**beautiful**___ sunset in the world!

The sunrise is ___**pretty**___.

— Sight Words —
Say each word. Trace it. Say the letter names.

twice   leave   drink

---

84 **VOCABULARY**

Character

A **character** is who a story is about.

Sam   dog   Cinderella

Write the names of three characters you like.

1. ___**Answers will vary.**___

2. _____

3. _____

— Sight Words —
Say each word. Trace it. Say the letter names.

found   they   clothes

---

86 **VOCABULARY**

Setting

The **setting** is where and when a story takes place.

home   beach

Write the names of three settings you know.

1. ___**Answers will vary.**___

2. _____

3. _____

— Sight Words —
Say each word. Trace it. Say the letter names.

before   eight   super

---

88 **VOCABULARY**

Plot

The **plot** includes the main things that happen in a story. A story plot has a beginning, a middle, and an end.

Beginning: A girl loses her cat.
Middle: A girl looks for her cat.
End: A girl finds her cat.

Write the plot of a story you know.

Beginning: ___**Answers will vary.**___

_____

Middle: _____

_____

End: _____

_____

— Sight Words —
Say each word. Trace it. Say the letter names.

woman   out   straight

---

90 **VOCABULARY**

Main Ideas

The **main ideas** are the most important facts in a text.

Book Title: Sharks
1. Live in the ocean.
2. Have sharp teeth.
3. Breathe through gills.

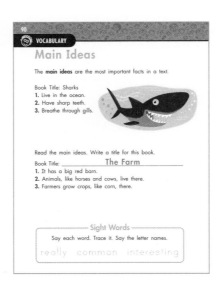

Read the main ideas. Write a title for this book.

Book Title: ___**The Farm**___
1. It has a big red barn.
2. Animals, like horses and cows, live there.
3. Farmers grow crops, like corn, there.

— Sight Words —
Say each word. Trace it. Say the letter names.

really   common   interesting